THE ESSENTIAL
Black Sabbath

Cover photo by Bob Gruen/Star File

ISBN 978-0-634-06251-3

HAL•LEONARD®
CORPORATION

7777 W. Bluemound Rd. P.O. Box 13819 Milwaukee, WI 53213

Visit Hal Leonard Online at
www.halleonard.com

Guitar Notation Legend

Guitar Music can be notated three different ways: on a *musical staff*, in *tablature*, and in *rhythm slashes*.

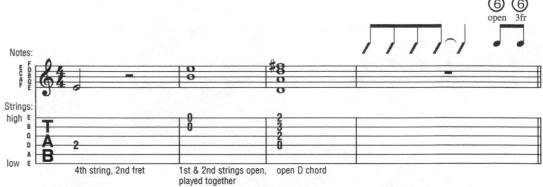

RHYTHM SLASHES are written above the staff. Strum chords in the rhythm indicated. Use the chord diagrams found at the top of the first page of the transcription for the appropriate chord voicings. Round noteheads indicate single notes.

THE MUSICAL STAFF shows pitches and rhythms and is divided by bar lines into measures. Pitches are named after the first seven letters of the alphabet.

TABLATURE graphically represents the guitar fingerboard. Each horizontal line represents a string, and each number represents a fret.

HALF-STEP BEND: Strike the note and bend up 1/2 step.

WHOLE-STEP BEND: Strike the note and bend up one step.

GRACE NOTE BEND: Strike the note and immediately bend up as indicated.

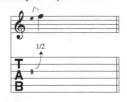

SLIGHT (MICROTONE) BEND: Strike the note and bend up 1/4 step.

BEND AND RELEASE: Strike the note and bend up as indicated, then release back to the original note. Only the first note is struck.

PRE-BEND: Bend the note as indicated, then strike it.

VIBRATO: The string is vibrated by rapidly bending and releasing the note with the fretting hand.

WIDE VIBRATO: The pitch is varied to a greater degree by vibrating with the fretting hand.

HAMMER-ON: Strike the first (lower) note with one finger, then sound the higher note (on the same string) with another finger by fretting it without picking.

PULL-OFF: Place both fingers on the notes to be sounded. Strike the first note and without picking, pull the finger off to sound the second (lower) note.

LEGATO SLIDE: Strike the first note and then slide the same fret-hand finger up or down to the second note. The second note is not struck.

SHIFT SLIDE: Same as legato slide, except the second note is struck.

TRILL: Very rapidly alternate between the notes indicated by continuously hammering on and pulling off.

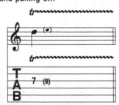

TAPPING: Hammer ("tap") the fret indicated with the pick-hand index or middle finger and pull off to the note fretted by the fret hand.

NATURAL HARMONIC: Strike the note while the fret-hand lightly touches the string directly over the fret indicated.

PINCH HARMONIC: The note is fretted normally and a harmonic is produced by adding the edge of the thumb or the tip of the index finger of the pick hand to the normal pick attack.

PICK SCRAPE: The edge of the pick is rubbed down (or up) the string, producing a scratchy sound.

MUFFLED STRINGS: A percussive sound is produced by laying the fret hand across the string(s) without depressing, and striking them with the pick hand.

PALM MUTING: The note is partially muted by the pick hand lightly touching the string(s) just before the bridge.

RAKE: Drag the pick across the strings indicated with a single motion.

TREMOLO PICKING: The note is picked as rapidly and continuously as possible.

VIBRATO BAR DIVE AND RETURN: The pitch of the note or chord is dropped a specified number of steps (in rhythm) then returned to the original pitch.

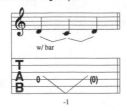

VIBRATO BAR SCOOP: Depress the bar just before striking the note, then quickly release the bar.

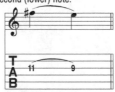

VIBRATO BAR DIP: Strike the note and then immediately drop a specified number of steps, then release back to the original pitch.

STRUM AND PICK PATTERNS

This chart contains the suggested strum and pick patterns that are referred to by number at the beginning
of each song in this book. The symbols ⊓ and ∨ in the strum patterns refer to down and up strokes, respectively.
The letters in the pick patterns indicate which right-hand fingers plays which strings.

p = thumb
i = index finger
m = middle finger
a = ring finger

For example; Pick Pattern 2
is played: thumb - index - middle - ring

Strum Patterns

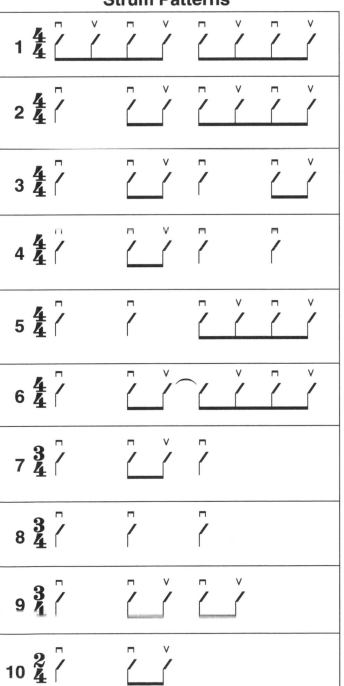

Pick Patterns

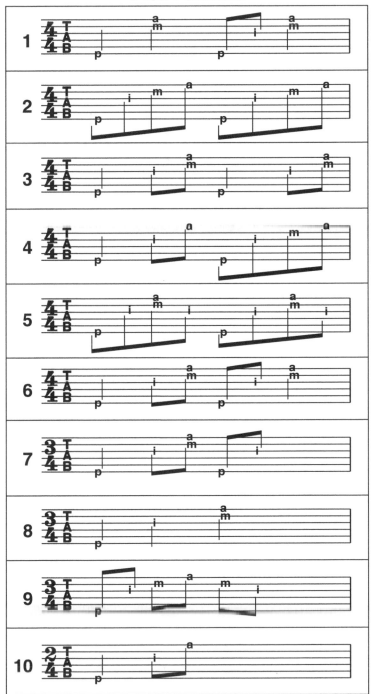

You can use the 3/4 Strum or Pick Patterns in songs written in compound meter (6/8, 9/8, 12/8, etc.).
For example, you can accompany a song in 6/8 by playing the 3/4 pattern twice in each measure.
The 4/4 Strum and Pick Patterns can be used for songs written in cut time (¢) by doubling the note
time values in the patterns. Each pattern would therefore last two measures in cut time.

Black Sabbath

Words and Music by Frank Iommi, John Osbourne, William Ward and Terence Butler

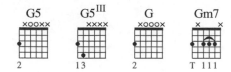

Strum Pattern: 3

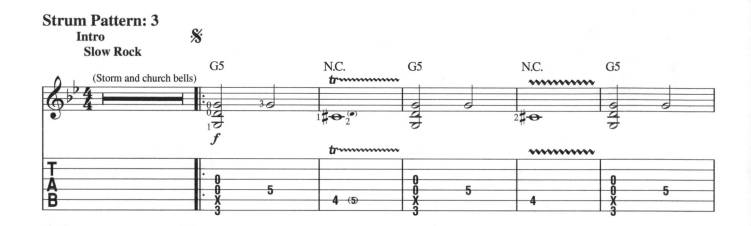

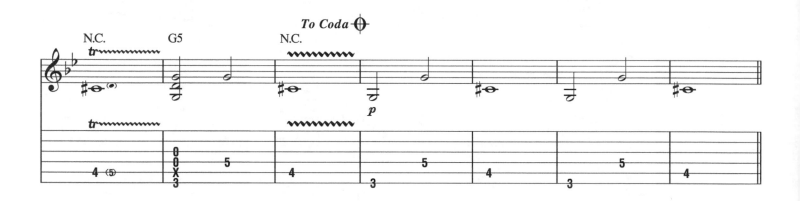

1. What is this ___ that stands ___ be - fore ___ me? ___
2. *See additional lyrics*

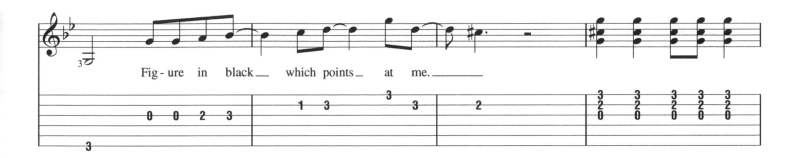

Fig - ure in black___ which points___ at me._____

Turn 'round   quick   and start___   to   run._____

2nd time, D.S. al Coda

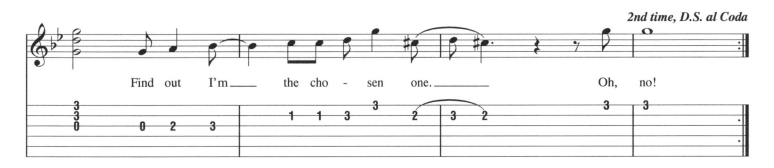

Find   out   I'm___   the   cho - sen   one._____   Oh,   no!

Coda

Interlude
Faster
G5   N.C.   *G5 III

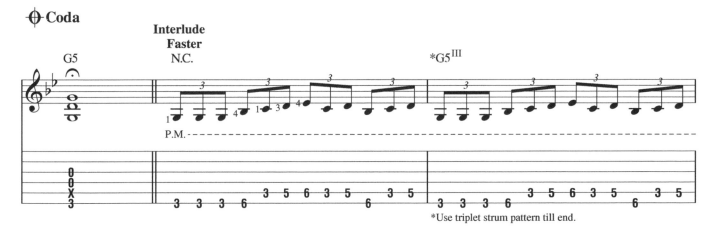

P.M. -

*Use triplet strum pattern till end.

Bridge
G5 III

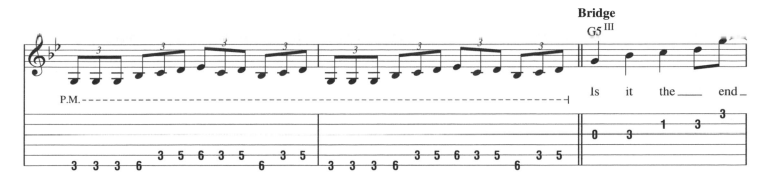

P.M. -   Is   it   the ___   end ___

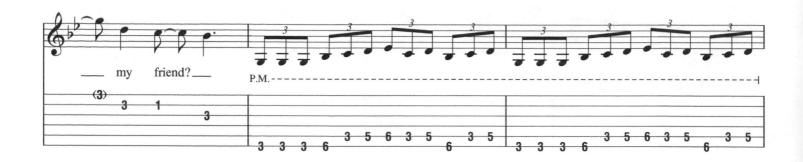

_____ my friend?_____ P.M.--

Sa - tan's com - in' round_____ the bend._____ P.M.-----------------------------------

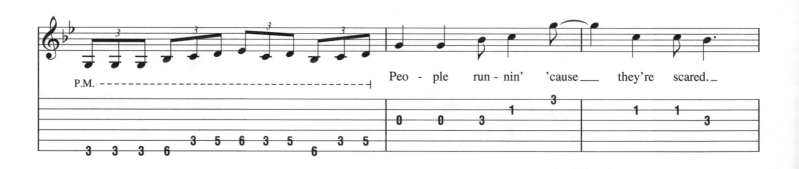

P.M.-- Peo - ple run - nin' 'cause_____ they're scared._____

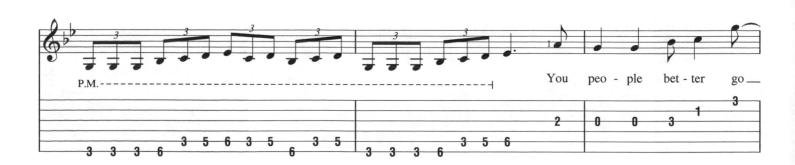

P.M.-- You peo - ple bet - ter go_____

— and be - ware. — No, no, please, no.

Guitar Solo

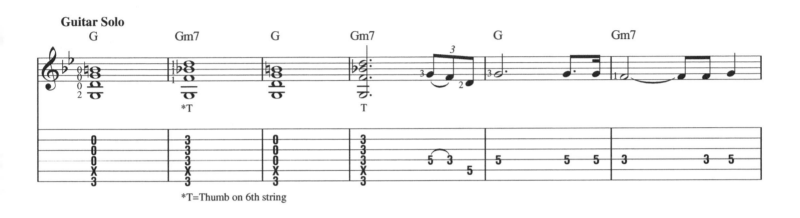

*T=Thumb on 6th string

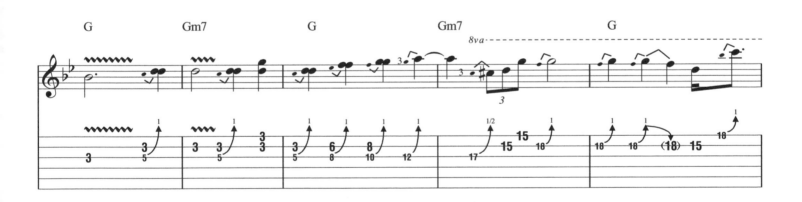

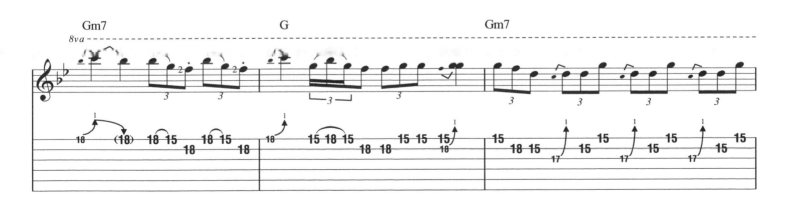

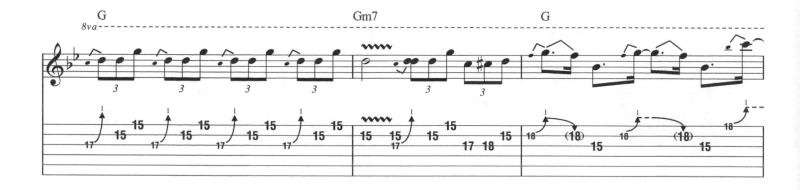

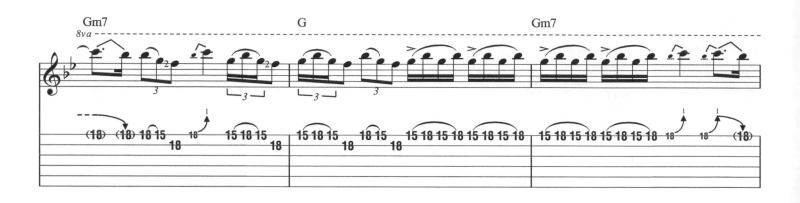

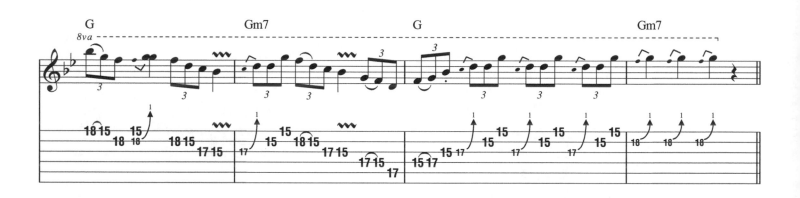

Outro

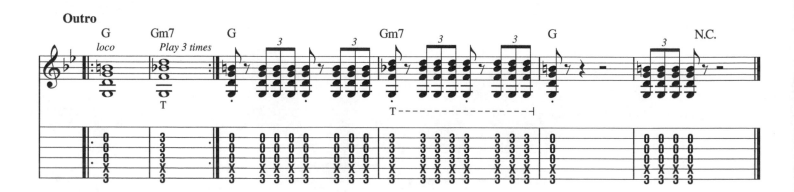

Additional Lyrics

2. Big black shape with eyes of fire,
   Telling people their desire.
   Satan's sitting there, he's smiling.
   Watches those flames get higher and higher.
   Oh, no, no, please God help me!

Children of the Grave

Words and Music by Frank Iommi, William Ward, John Osbourne and Terence Butler

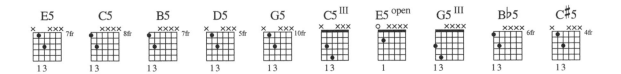

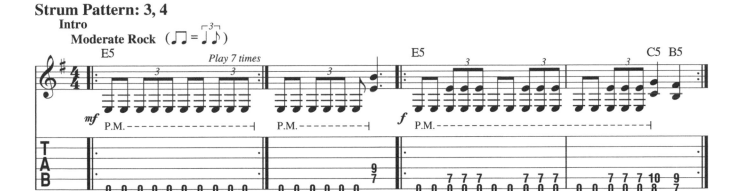

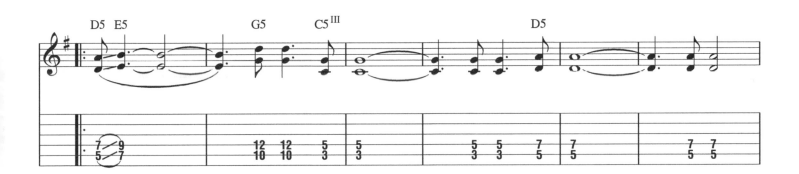

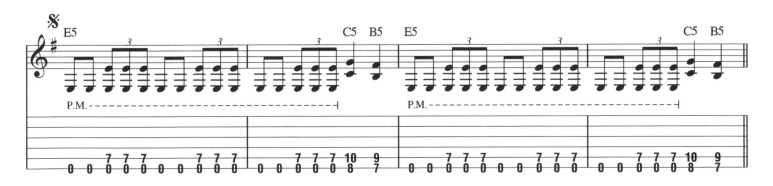

1. Rev - o - lu - tion in _____ their minds, _____ the chil - dren start _____ to march
2., 3. *See additional lyrics*

a - gainst the world__ in which they have to live__ in. Oh, the

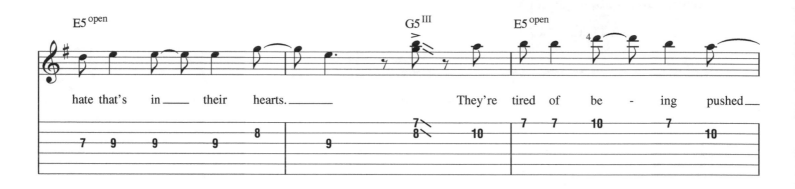

hate that's in__ their hearts._____ They're tired of be - ing pushed__

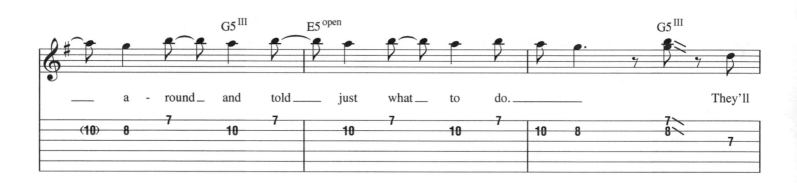

__ a - round__ and told__ just what__ to do._____ They'll

3rd time, to Coda ⊕

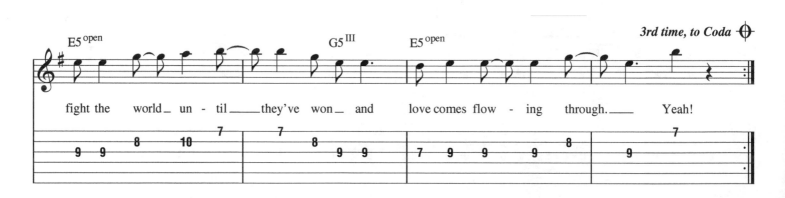

fight the world__ un - til __they've won__ and love comes flow - ing through.__ Yeah!

Interlude

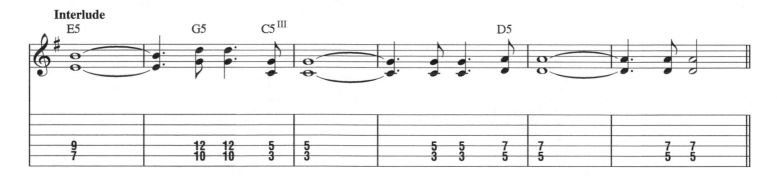

10

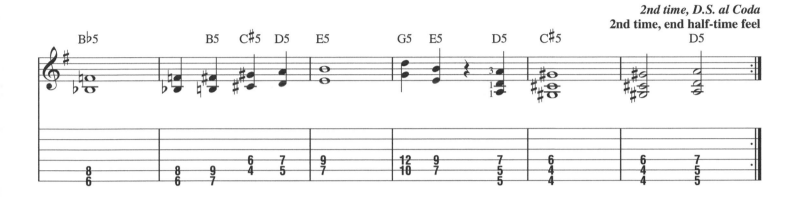

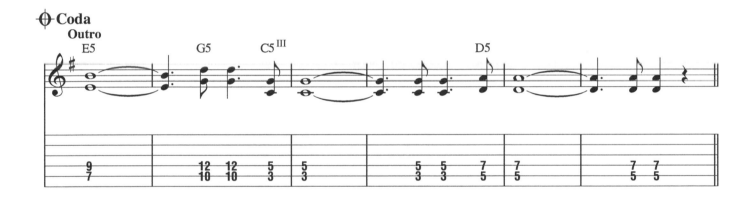

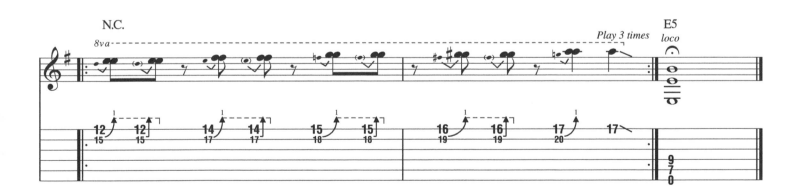

Additional Lyrics

2. Children of tomorrow live
   In the tears that fall today.
   Will the sunrise of tomorrow
   Bring in peace in any way?
   Must the world live
   In the shadow of atomic fear?
   Can they win the fight for peace
   Or will they disappear? Yeah!

3. So, you children of the world,
   Listen to what I say.
   If you want a better place to live in,
   Spread the words today.
   Show the world that love is still alive.
   You must be brave,
   Or you children of today
   Are children of the grave. Yeah!

Death Mask

Music by Frank Iommi, William Ward, John Osbourne and Terence Butler

Strum Pattern: 1, 2

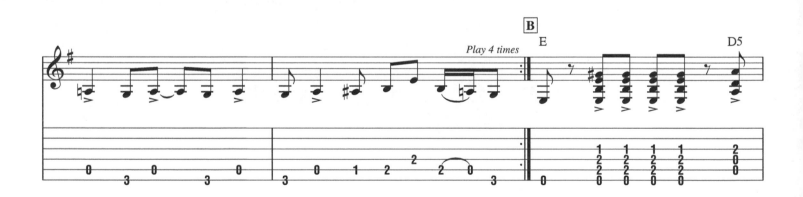

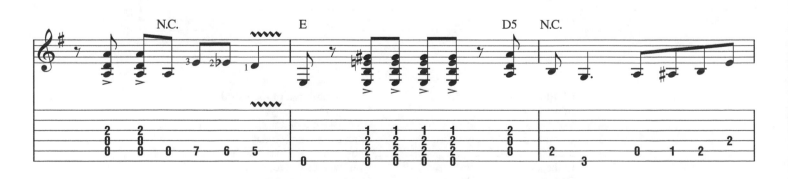

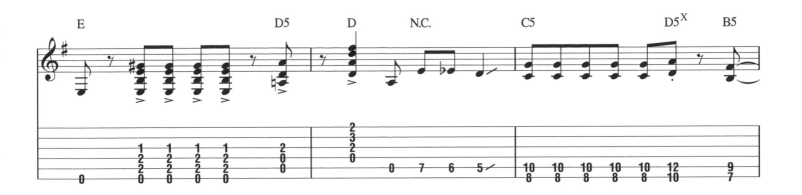

Segue into "Into the Void"

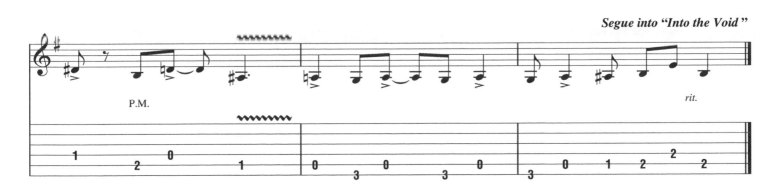

Into the Void

Words and Music by Frank Iommi, William Ward, John Osbourne and Terence Butler

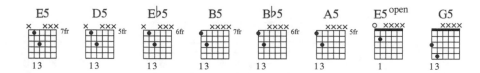

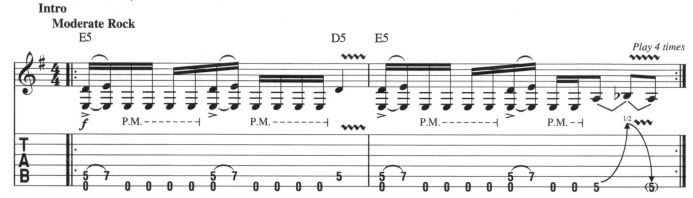

Strum Pattern: 1, 4

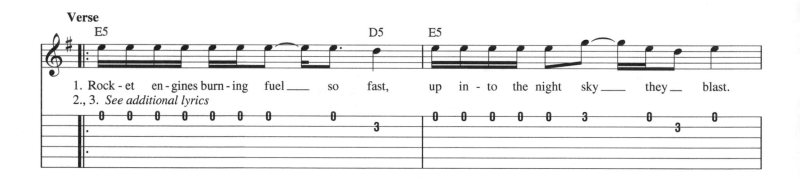

1. Rock - et en - gines burn - ing fuel ___ so fast, up in - to the night sky ___ they ___ blast.
2., 3. *See additional lyrics*

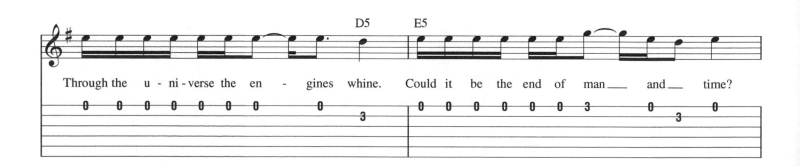

Through the u - ni - verse the en - gines whine. Could it be the end of man ___ and ___ time?

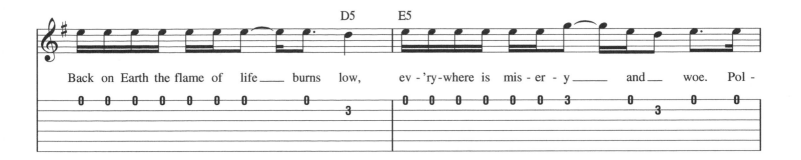

Back on Earth the flame of life____ burns low, ev -'ry-where is mis - er - y____ and__ woe. Pol -

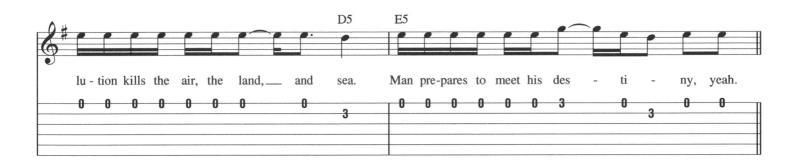

lu - tion kills the air, the land,___ and sea. Man pre-pares to meet his des - ti - ny, yeah.

Interlude

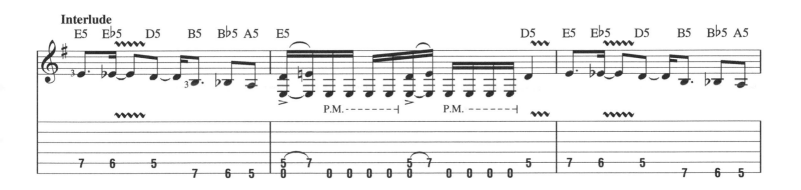

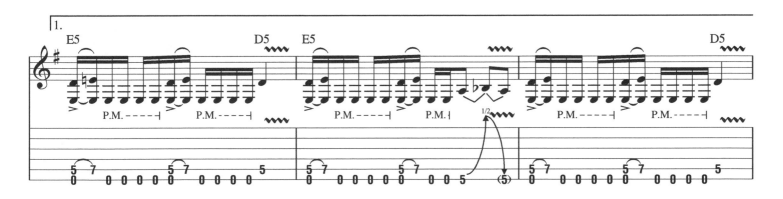

To Coda ⊕ **2.** **Faster**
Double-time feel

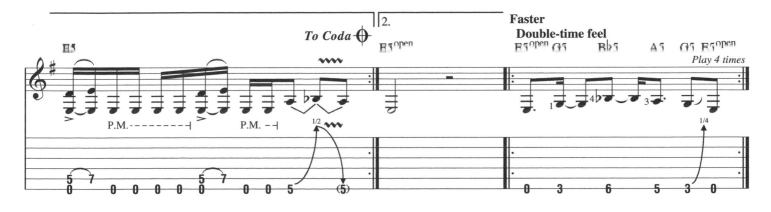

Play 4 times

Bridge

Free - dom fight - ers sent out to the sun. Es - cape from brain-washed minds

and pol - lu - tion. Leave the Earth to all its sin and hate.

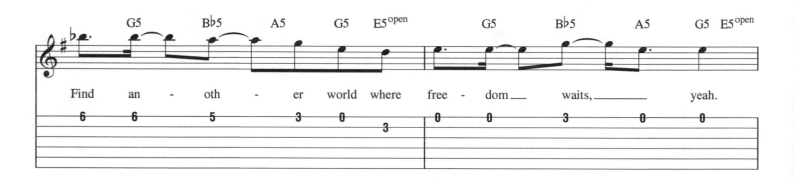

Find an - oth - er world where free - dom waits, yeah.

D.C al Coda
(take 1st ending)
End double-time feel

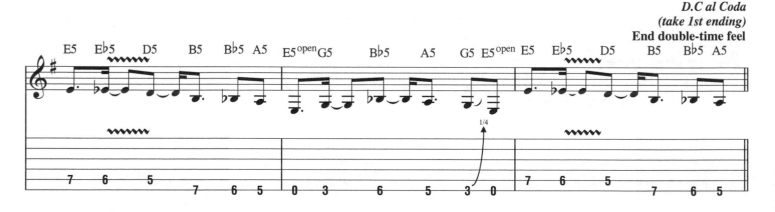

Coda
Guitar Solo

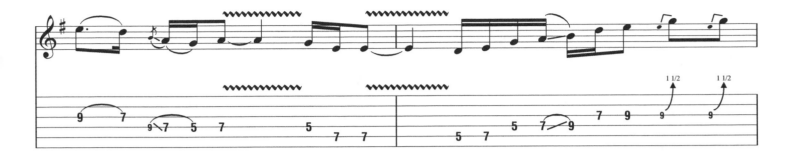

Interlude

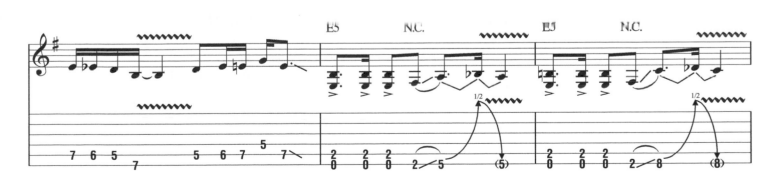

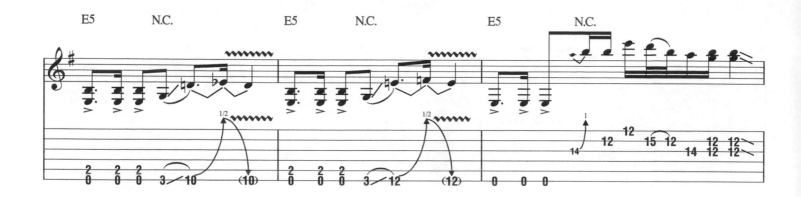

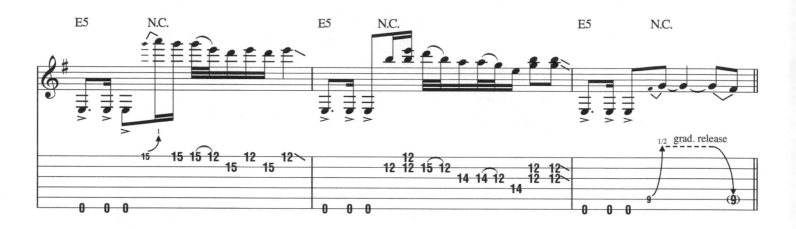

Outro

Additional Lyrics

2. Rocket engines burning fuel so fast,
Up into the black sky so vast.
Burning metal through the atmosphere.
Earth remains in worry, hate and fear.
With the hateful battles raging on,
Rockets flying to the glowing sun.
Through the empires of eternal void,
Freedom from the final suicide.

3. Past the stars in fields of ancient void,
Through the shields of darkness where they find
Love upon a land, a world unknown,
Where the sons of freedom make their home.
Leave the Earth to Satan and his slaves,
Leave them to their future in their graves.
Make a home where love is there to stay,
Peace and happiness in ev'ry day.

N.I.B.

Words and Music by Frank Iommi, Terence Butler, William Ward and John Osbourne

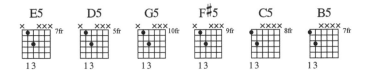

Strum Pattern: 1

1. Some peo - ple say my love can - not be true.
2. – 5. *See additional lyrics*

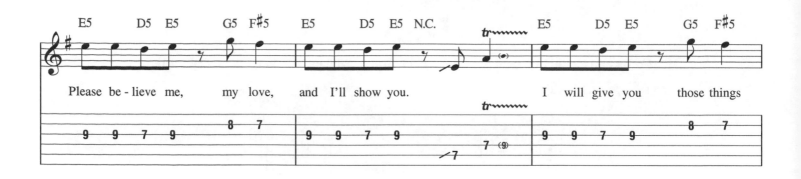

Please be-lieve me, my love, and I'll show you. I will give you those things

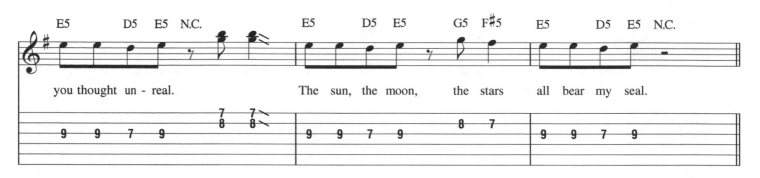

you thought un - real. The sun, the moon, the stars all bear my seal.

2nd time, to Coda 1 ⊕
3rd time, to Coda 2 ⊕

1. **Interlude**

2.

Bridge

Your love for me has just got to be real

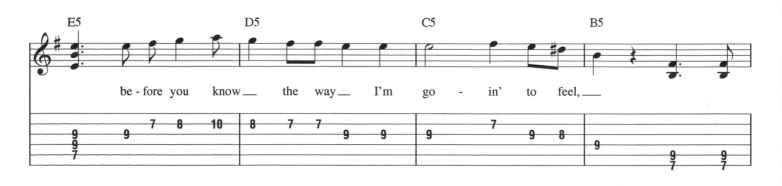

be-fore you know the way I'm go - in' to feel,

D.S. al Coda 1
(take 1st ending)
2nd time, D.S. al Coda 2
(take 1st ending)

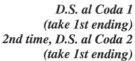

I'm go - in' to feel, __ I'm go - in' to feel. _____

Coda 1
Guitar Solo

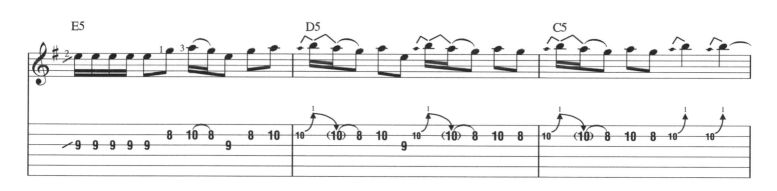

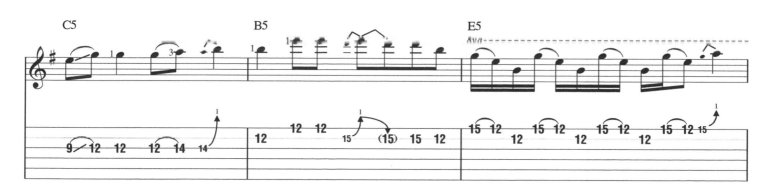

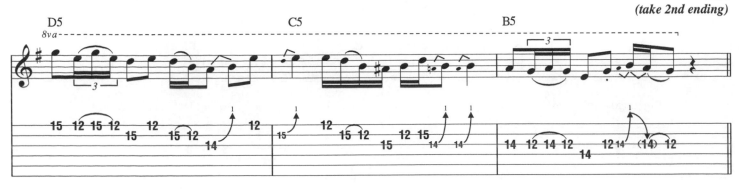

✛ Coda 2
Outro-Guitar Solo

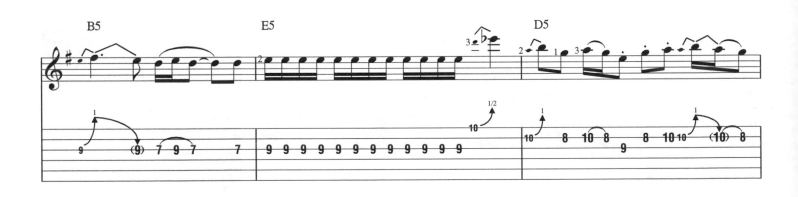

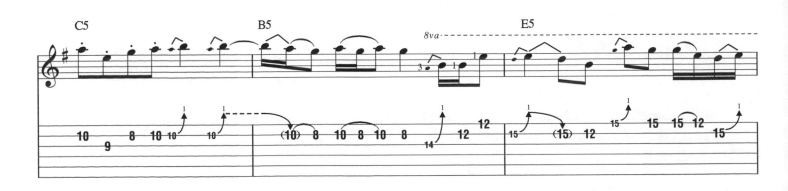

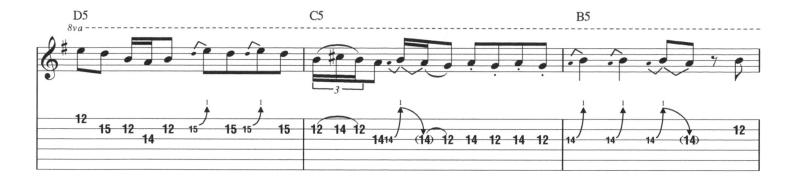

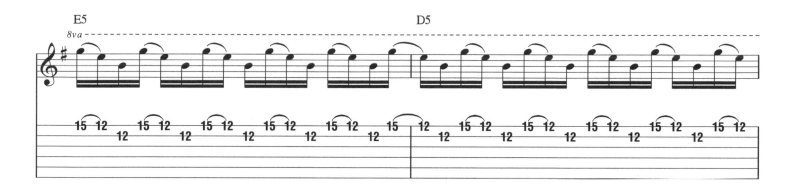

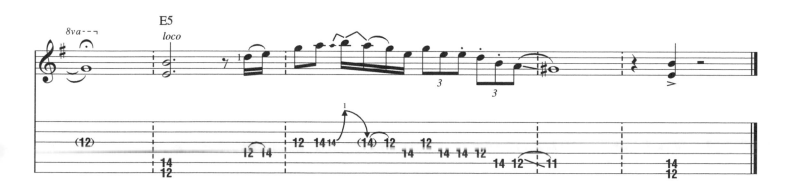

Additional Lyrics

2., 4. Follow me now and you will not regret
Living the life you led before we met.
You are the first to have this love of mine,
Forever with me 'til the end of time.

3., 5. Now I have you with me under my pow'r.
Our love grows stronger now with ev'ry hour.
Look into my eyes, you'll see who I am.
My name is Lucifer, please take my hand.

Electric Funeral

Words and Music by Frank Iommi, John Osbourne, William Ward and Terence Butler

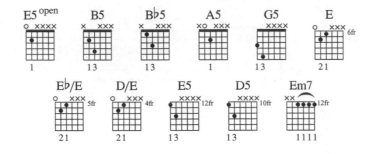

Strum Pattern: 1, 5

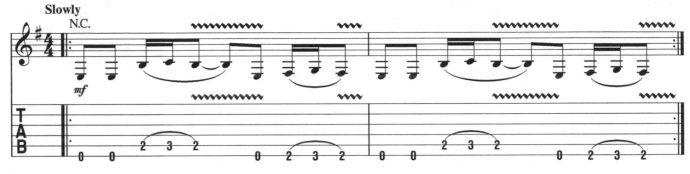

Verse

1. Re - flex in the sky,__ warn you you're gon-na die.__ Storm com-ing you bet-ter hide__
2., 3. *See additional lyrics*

from the a - tom - ic tide.__ Flash - es in the sky__ turns hous - es in - to sty.__

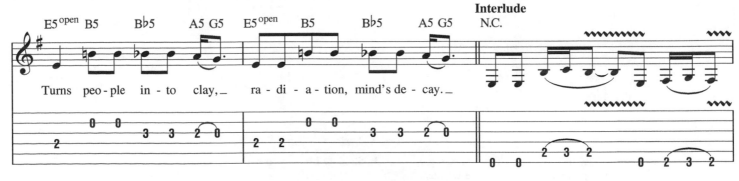

Turns peo - ple in - to clay,__ ra - di - a - tion, mind's de - cay.__

Interlude

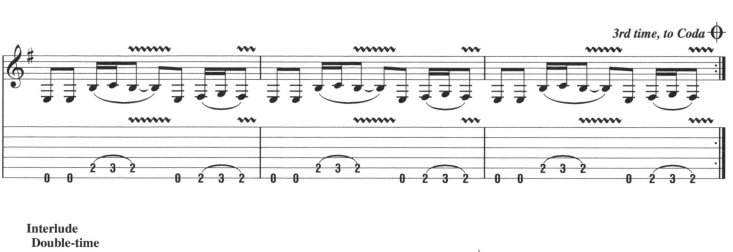

Interlude
Double-time

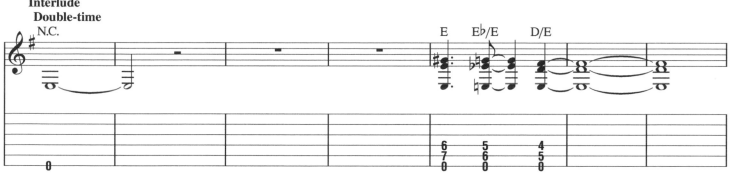

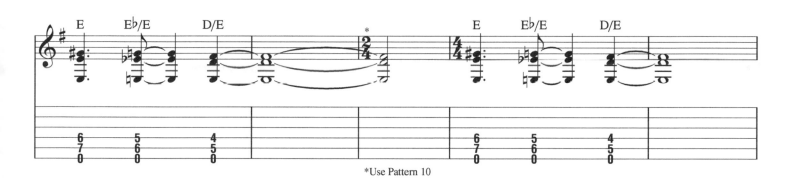

*Use Pattern 10

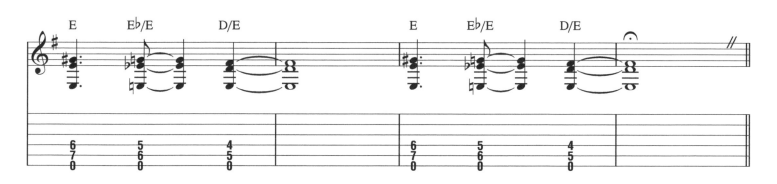

Bridge
Moderately

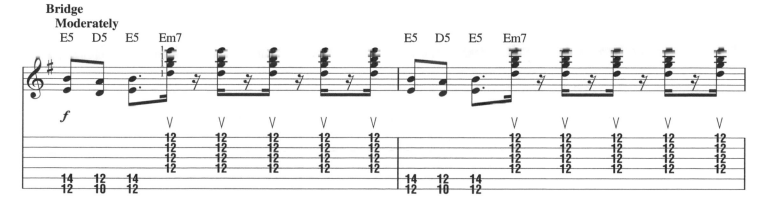

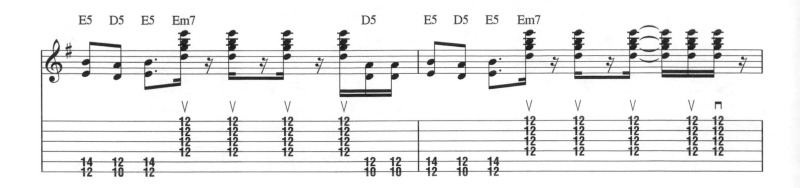

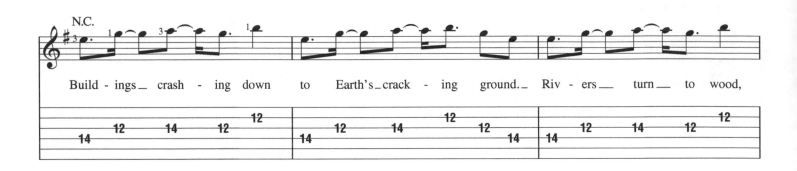

Build - ings__ crash - ing down   to   Earth's__ crack - ing   ground.__   Riv - ers__   turn__   to   wood,

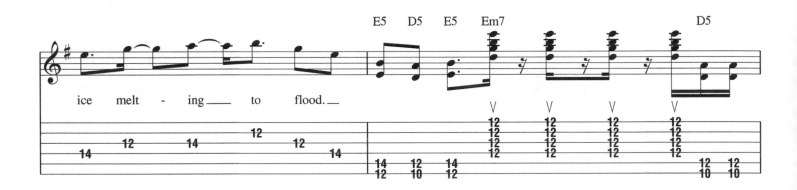

ice   melt - ing____   to   flood.__

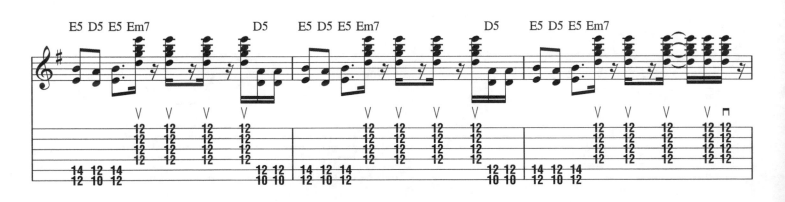

Earth   lies__   in__   death   bed,   clouds   cry__   for__   the   dead.__   Ter - ri - fy - ing   rain

ease the __ burn - ing pain. __ 'Lec - tric __ fun - n'ral. 'Lec - tric __ fun - n'ral.

'Lec - tric __ fun - n'ral. 'Lec - tric __ fun - n'ral.

D.C. al Coda
Tempo I
(Drums)

Coda
Outro

Repeat and fade

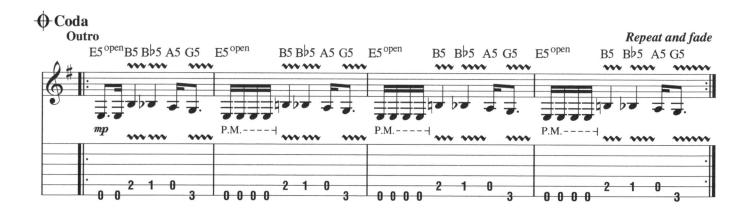

Additional Lyrics

2. Robot minds of robot slaves
Lead them to atomic rage.
Plastic flowers, melting sun,
Fading moon falls apart.
Dying world of radiation,
Victims of mad frustration.
Burning globe of obscene fire,
Like electric funeral pyre.

3. And so, in the sky
Shines the electric eye.
Supernatural king
Takes Earth under his wing.
Heaven's golden chorus sings,
Hell's angels flap their wings.
Evil souls fall to Hell,
Ever trapped in burning cell.

Iron Man

Words and Music by Frank Iommi, John Osbourne, William Ward and Terence Butler

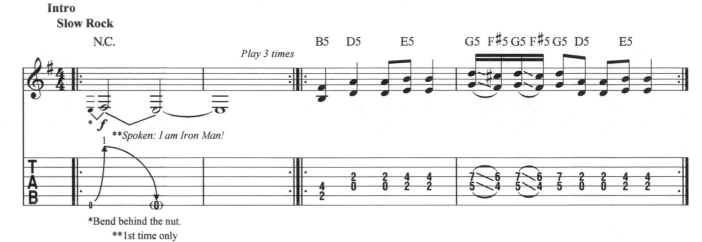

Strum Pattern: 2, 5

Intro
Slow Rock

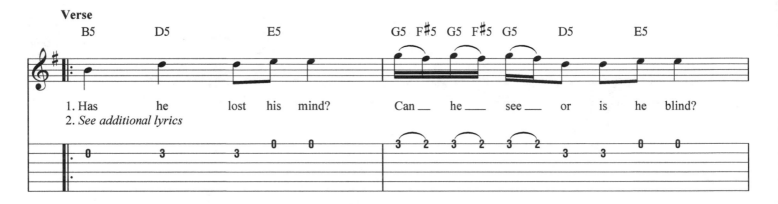

*Bend behind the nut.
**1st time only

Verse

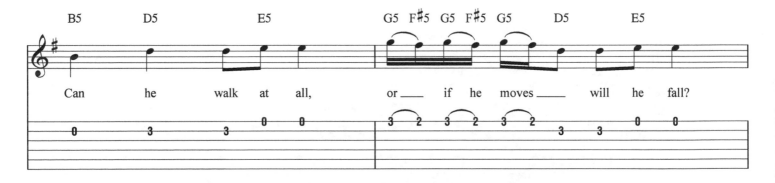

1. Has he lost his mind? Can he see or is he blind?
2. *See additional lyrics*

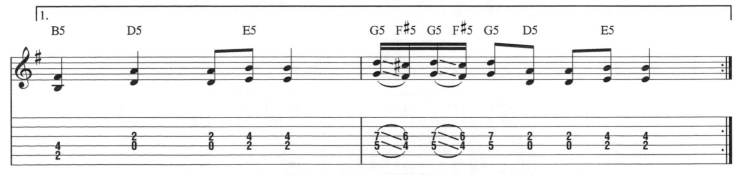

Can he walk at all, or if he moves will he fall?

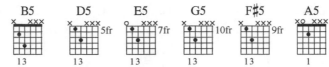

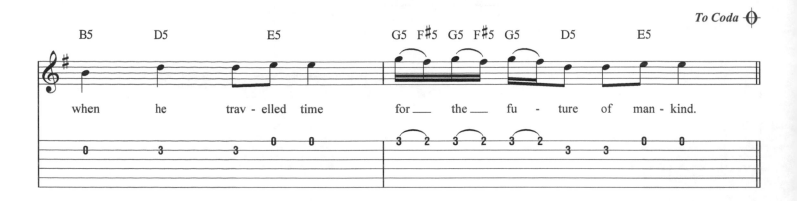

when he trav-elled time for __ the __ fu - ture of man - kind.

Bridge

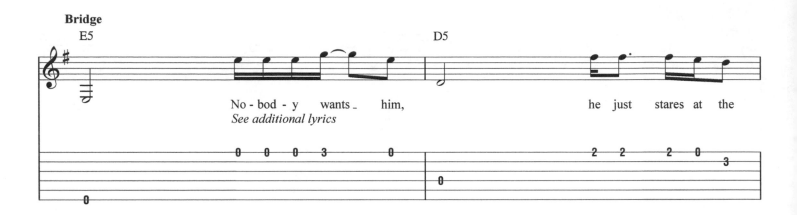

No - bod - y wants _ him, he just stares at the
See additional lyrics

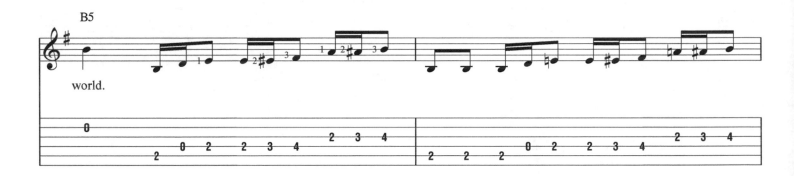

world.

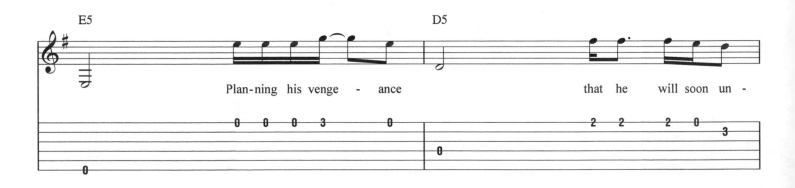

Plan-ning his venge - ance that he will soon un -

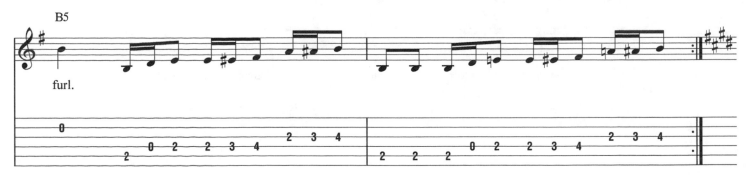

furl.

Interlude
Double-time feel

End double-time feel

D.S. al Coda

⊕ **Coda**

Repeat and fade

Additional Lyrics

2. Is he live or dead?
   I see thoughts within his head.
   We'll just pass him there.
   Why should we even care?

4. Now the time is here
   For Iron Man to spread fear.
   Vengeance from the grave,
   Kills the people he once saved.

Bridge Nobody wants him, they just turn their heads.
   Nobody helps him, now he has his revenge.

5. Heavy boots of lead
   Fill his victims full of dread.
   Running as fast as they can.
   Iron Man lives again!

Jack the Stripper

Words and Music by Frank Iommi, John Osbourne, Terence Butler and William Ward

Strum Pattern: 2, 5

Fairies Wear Boots
(Interpolating Jack the Stripper)

Words and Music by Frank Iommi, John Osbourne, William Ward and Terence Butler

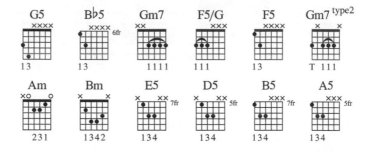

Strum Pattern: 1, 6

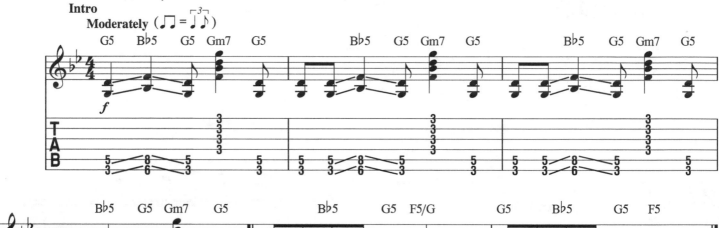

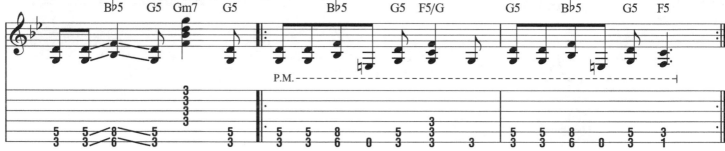

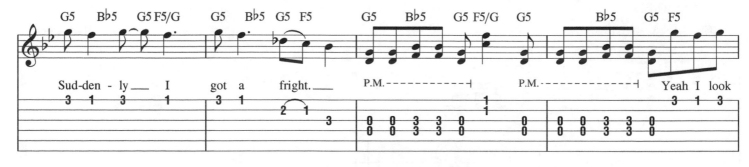

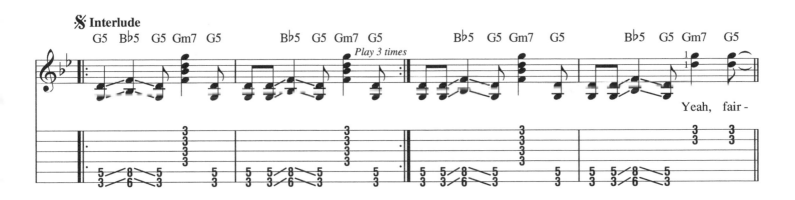

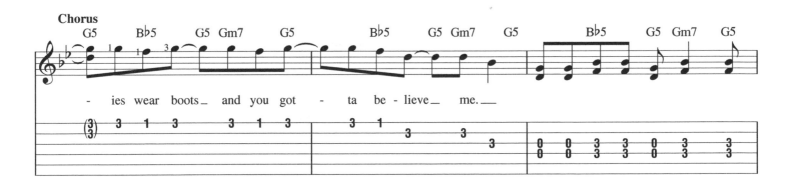

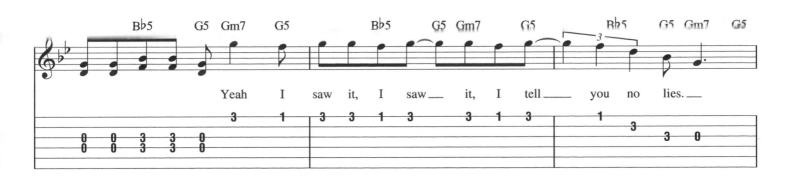

Yeah fair - ies wear boots_ and you got-

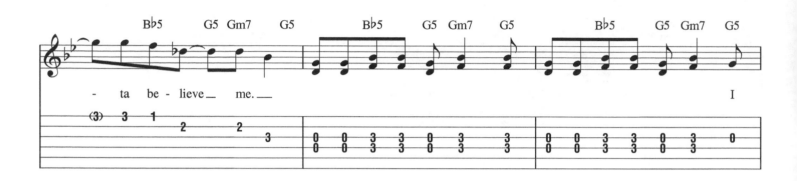

- ta be - lieve_ me. _   I

To Coda ⊕

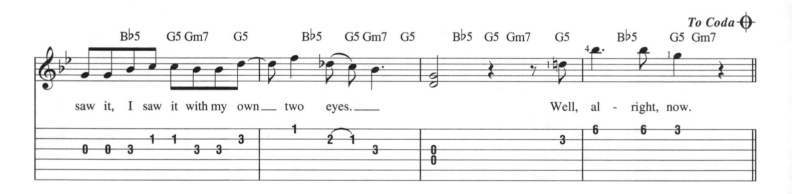

saw it, I saw it with my own_ two eyes.___   Well, al - right, now.

Guitar Solo

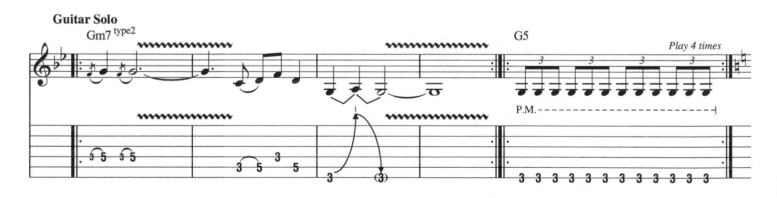

"Jack the Stripper"
Slower

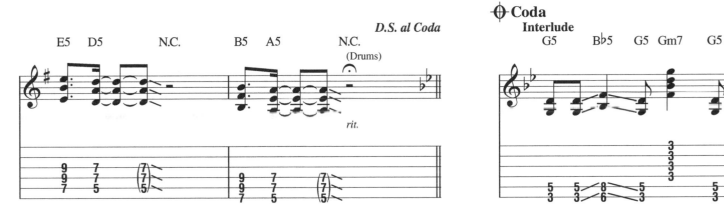

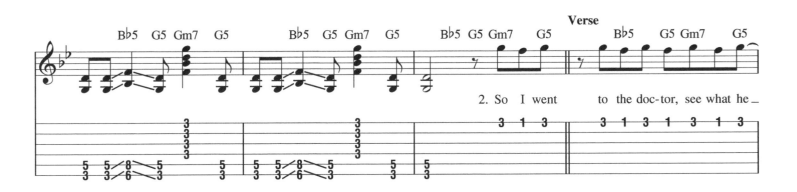

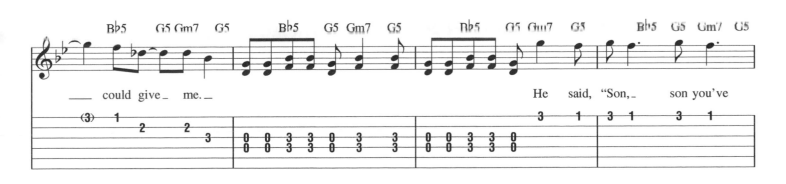

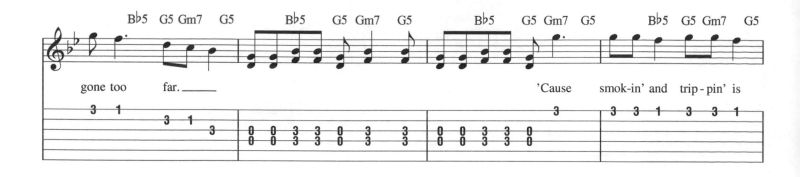

gone too   far. _____   'Cause   smok-in' and   trip-pin' is

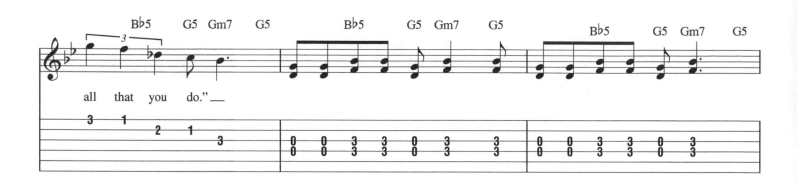

all   that   you   do." _____

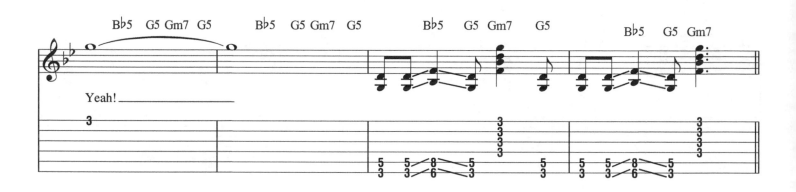

Yeah! _____

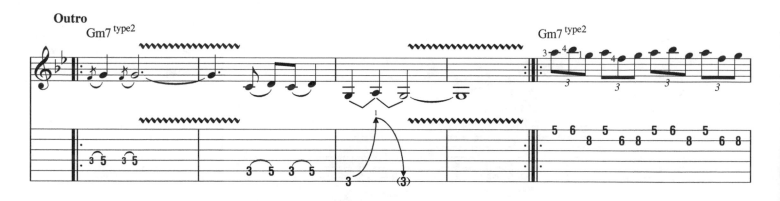

Outro

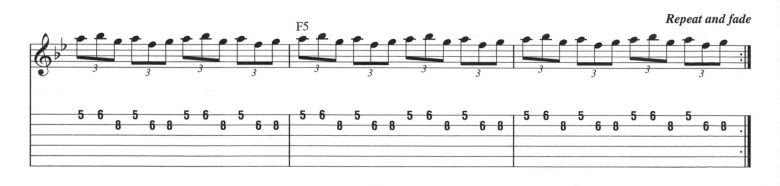

Repeat and fade

Step Up

Music by Frank Iommi, William Ward, John Osbourne and Terence Butler

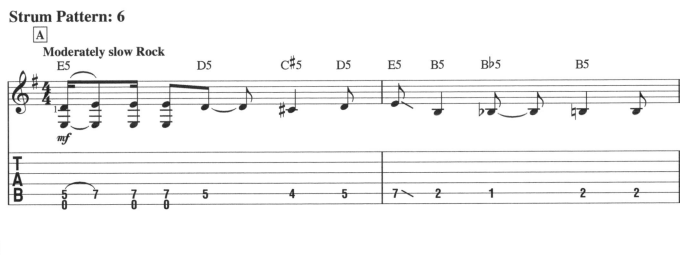

Strum Pattern: 6

Segue into "Lord of This World"

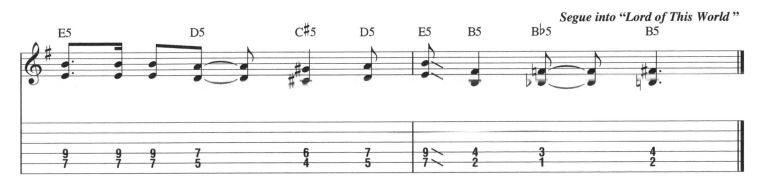

Lord of This World

Words and Music by Frank Iommi, William Ward, John Osbourne and Terence Butler

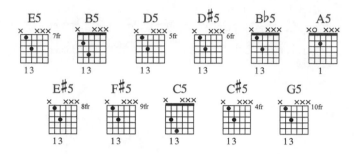

Strum Pattern: 5

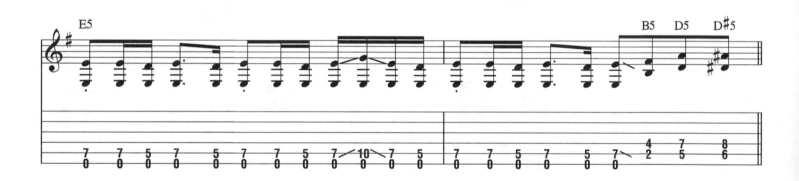

1. You're search-ing for your mind, don't know where to start. _____ Can't find the key _ to fit the
2., 3. *See additional lyrics*

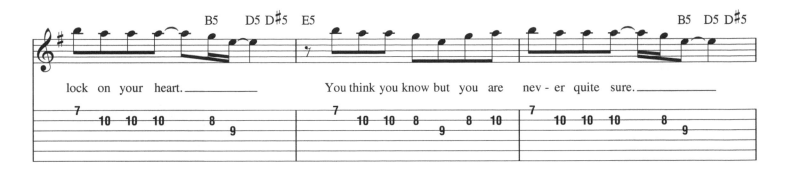

lock on your heart._____ You think you know but you are nev-er quite sure._____

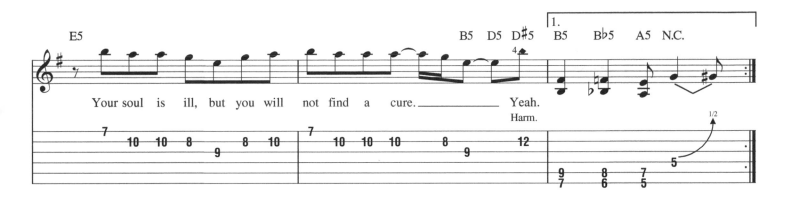

Your soul is ill, but you will not find a cure._____ Yeah.

Harm.

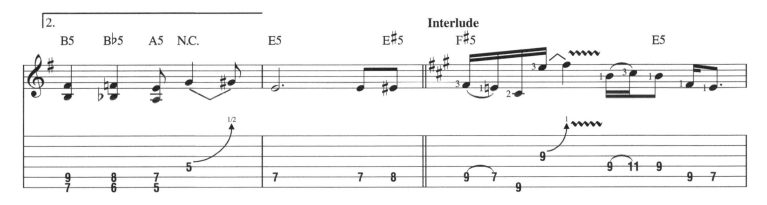

Interlude

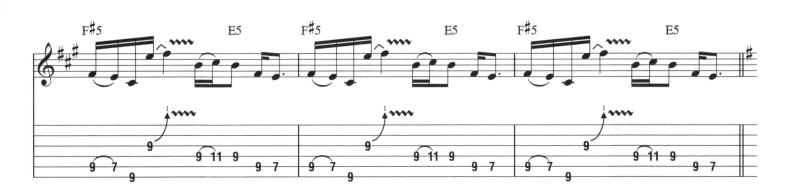

Guitar Solo

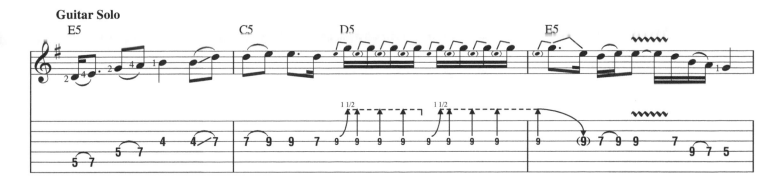

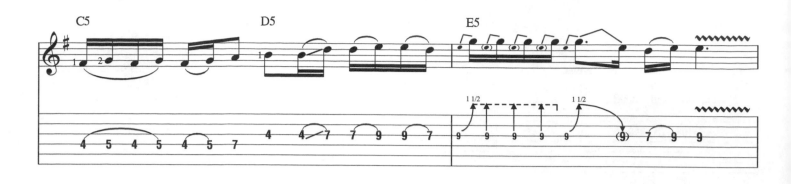

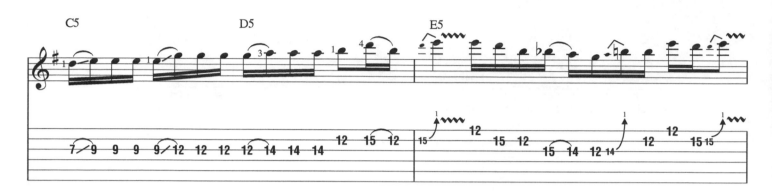

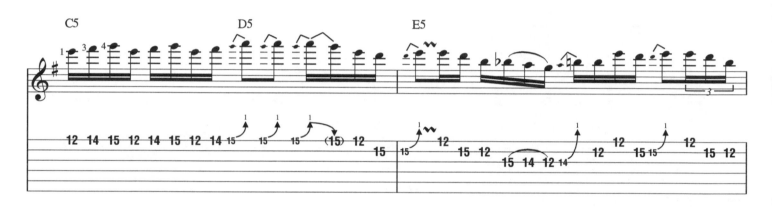

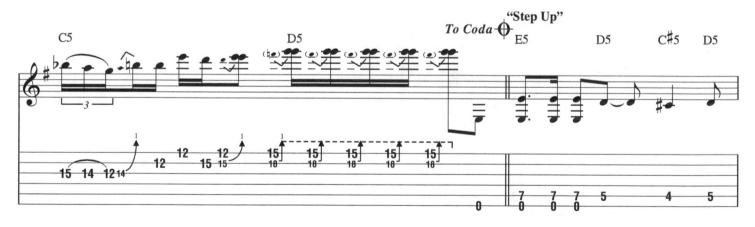

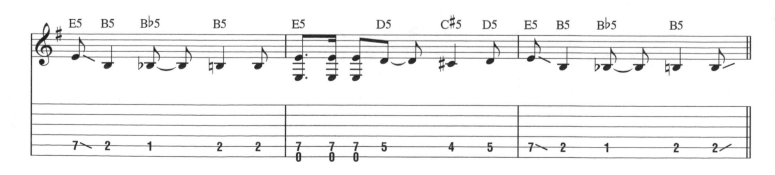

Bridge

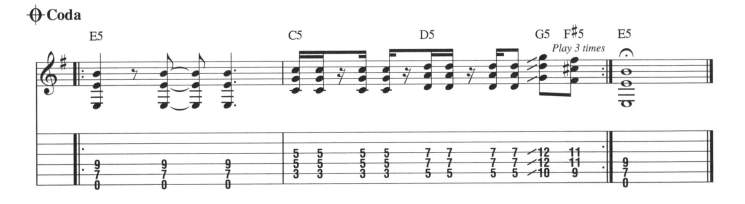

Additional Lyrics

2. Your world was made for you
By someone above.
But you choose evil ways
Instead of love.
You made me master of the world
Where you exist.
The soul I took from you
Was not even missed. Yeah.

3. You think you're innocent,
You've nothing to fear.
You don't know me, you say,
But isn't it clear?
You turn to me in all your
Worldly greed and pride.
But will you turn to me
When it's your turn to die? Yeah.

Paranoid

Words and Music by Anthony Iommi, John Osbourne, William Ward and Terence Butler

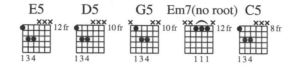

Interlude

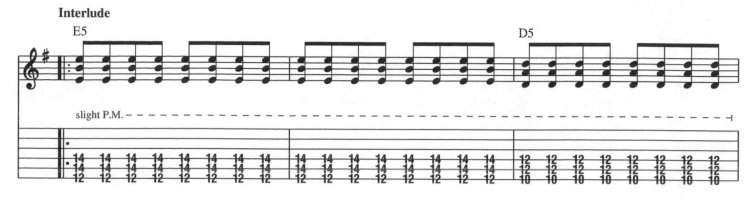

Verse

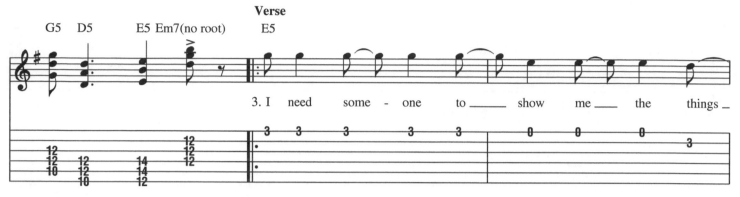

3. I need some-one to ____ show me ____ the things ____

____ in life ____ that I can't find. I can't see ____ the things ____

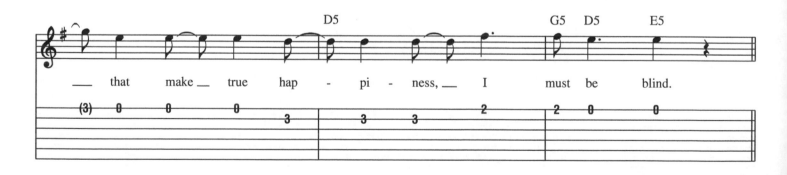

____ that make ____ true hap - pi - ness, ____ I must be blind.

Guitar Solo

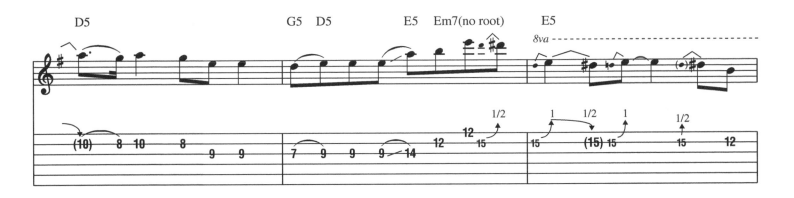

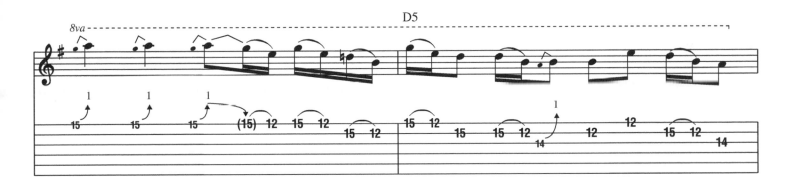

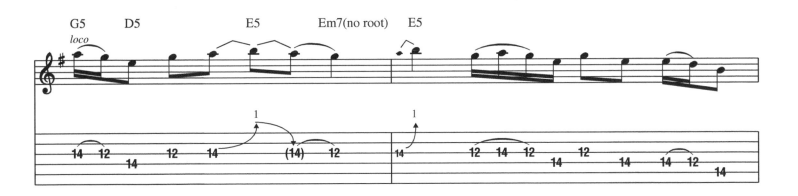

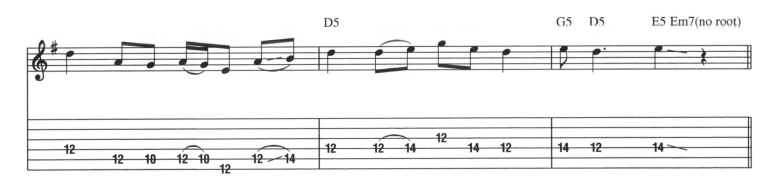

Interlude

⊕ **Coda**

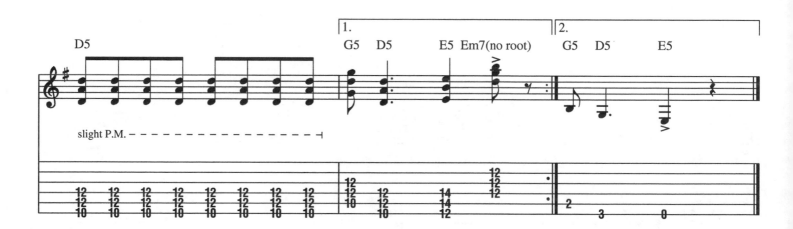

Additional Lyrics

4. Make a joke and I will sigh
   And you will laugh and I will cry.
   Happiness I cannot feel
   And love to me is so unreal.

5. And so as you hear these words
   Telling you now of my state.
   I tell you to enjoy life,
   I wish I could but it's too late.

Snowblind

Words and Music by Frank Iommi, Terence Butler, William Ward and John Osbourne

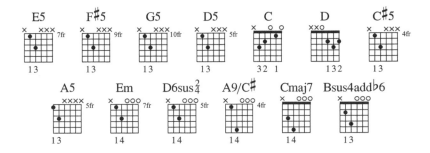

Strum Pattern: 4, 6

Intro
Moderate Rock

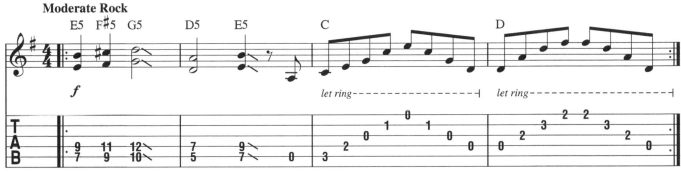

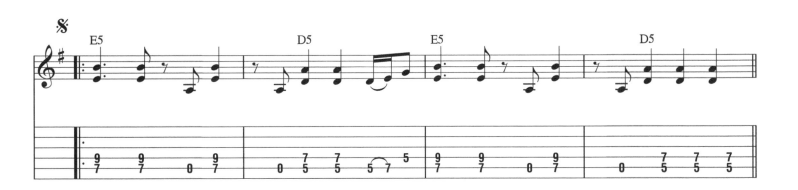

Verse

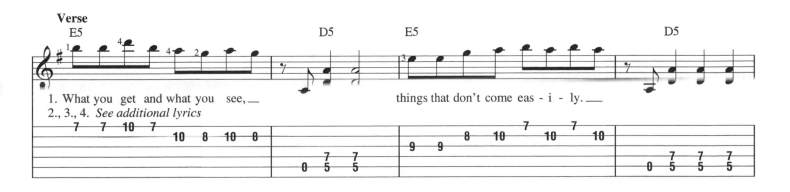

1. What you get and what you see, __
2., 3., 4. *See additional lyrics*

things that don't come eas - i - ly. __

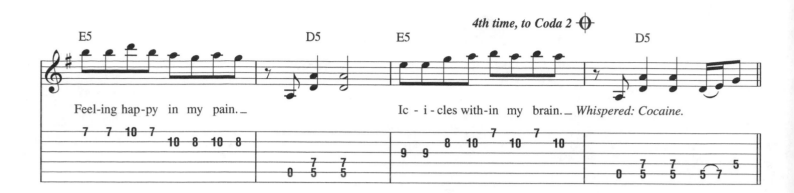

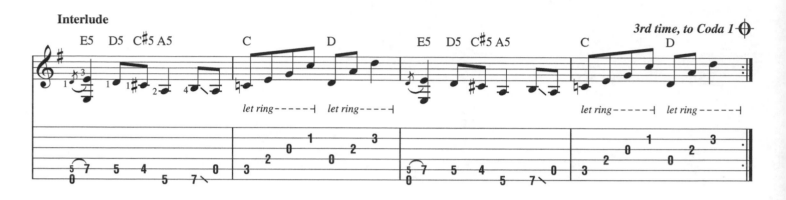

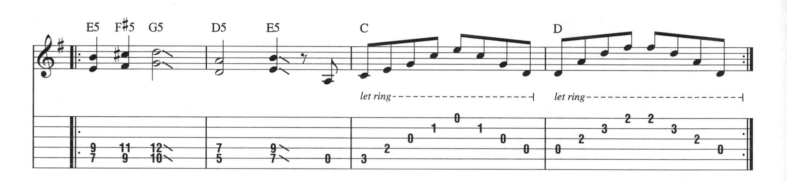

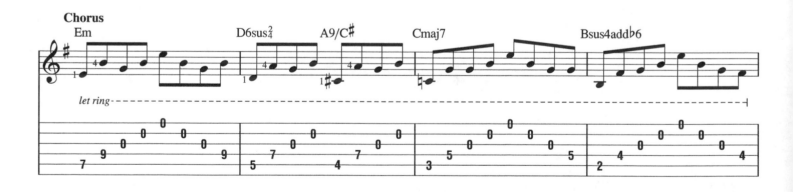

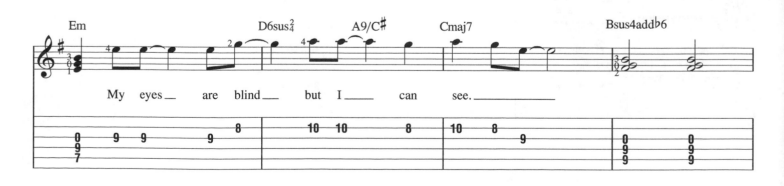

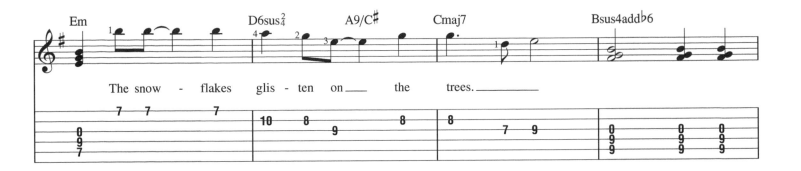

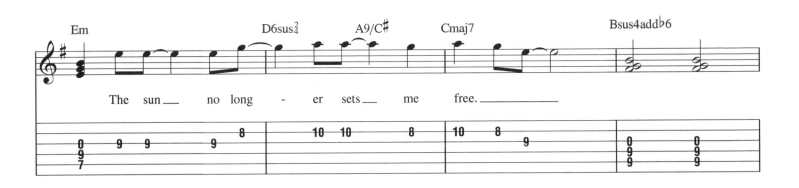

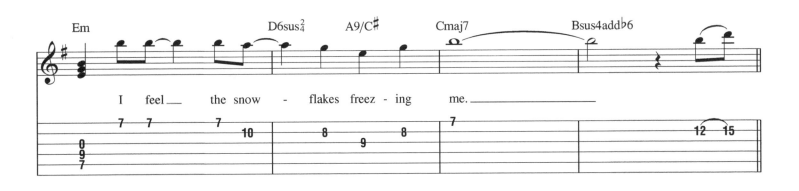

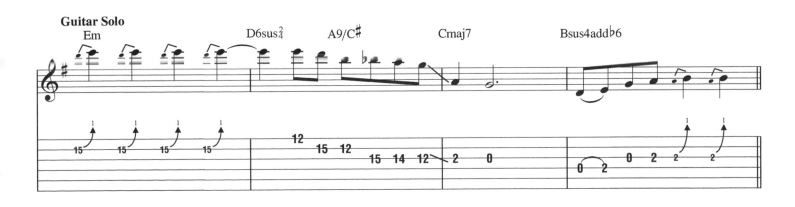

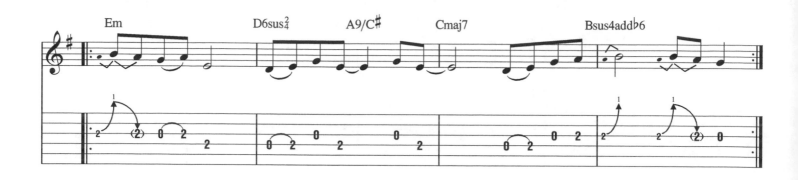

D.S. al Coda 1

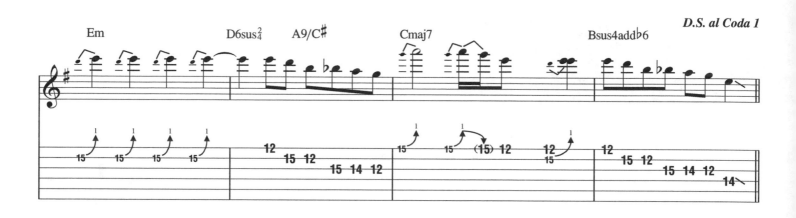

Don't you think I know what I'm do - - ing?   Don't tell me that it's do-ing me wrong. __

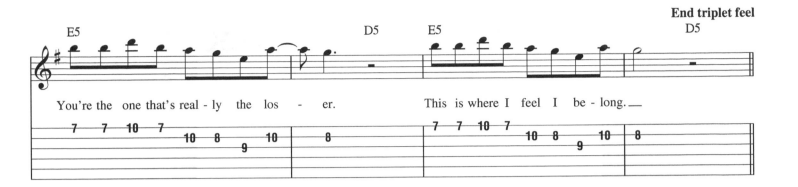

You're the one that's real - ly the los - er. This is where I feel I be - long. ___

Interlude

D.S. al Coda 2

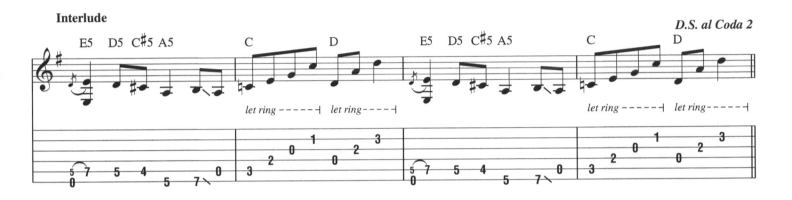

let ring - - - - - - ┤ let ring - - - - - ┤ *let ring - - - - - - ┤ let ring - - - - - ┤*

⊕ **Coda 2**

Outro-Guitar Solo

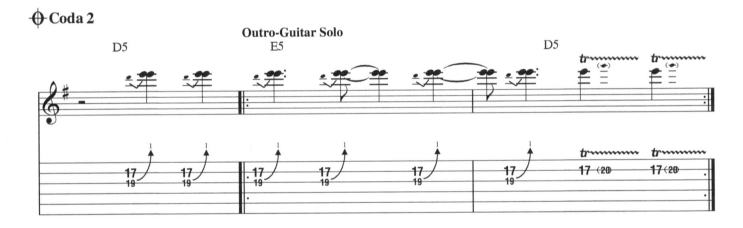

Repeat and fade

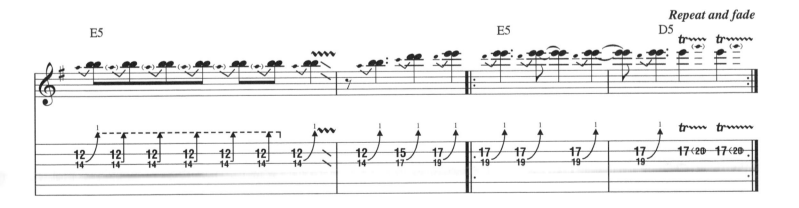

Additional Lyrics

2. Something blowing in my head,
   Winds of ice that soon will spread
   There to freeze my very soul.
   Makes me happy, makes me cold.

3. Let the winter sun shine on,
   Let me feel the frost of dawn.
   Fills my dreams with flakes of snow,
   Soon I'll feel the chilling glow.

4. Crystal world with winter flowers
   Turn my days to frozen hours.
   Lying snowblind in the sun,
   Will my ice age ever come?

Sabbath, Bloody Sabbath

Words and Music by Frank Iommi, John Osbourne, William Ward and Terence Butler

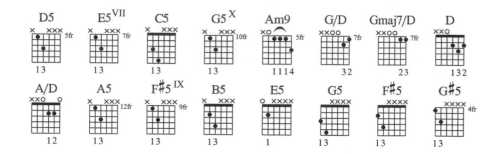

Strum Pattern: 3

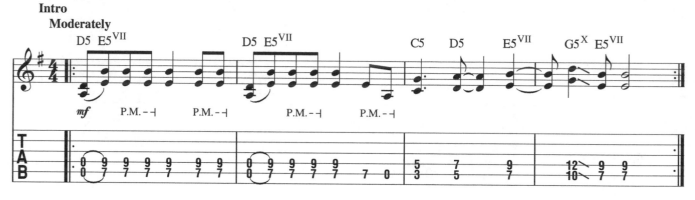

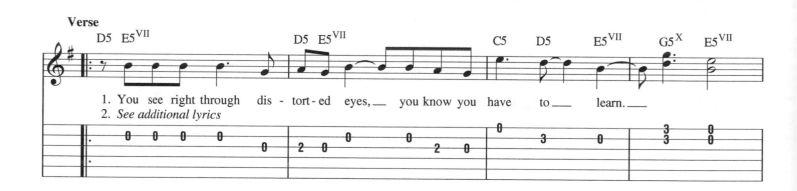

1. You see right through dis-tort-ed eyes,__ you know you have to__ learn.__
2. *See additional lyrics*

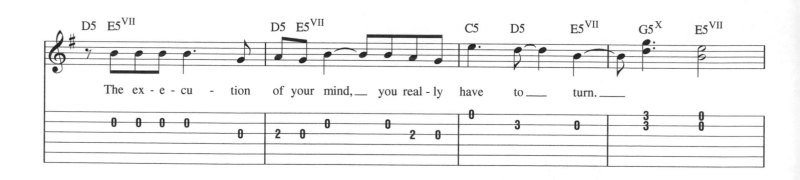

The ex-e-cu-tion of your mind,__ you real-ly have to__ turn.__

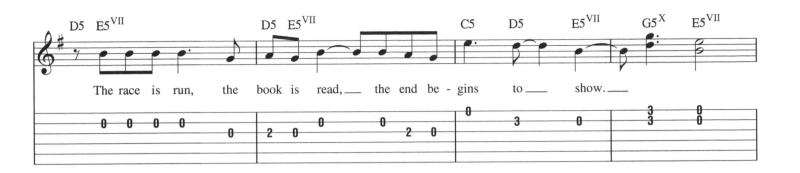

The race is run, the book is read,___ the end be-gins to ___ show.___

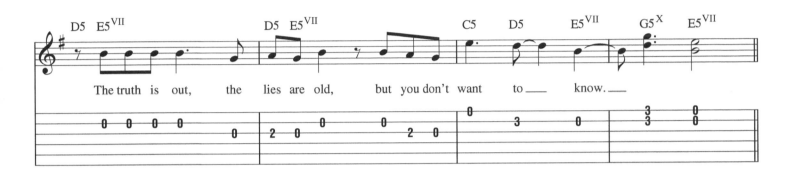

The truth is out, the lies are old, but you don't want to ___ know.___

Bridge

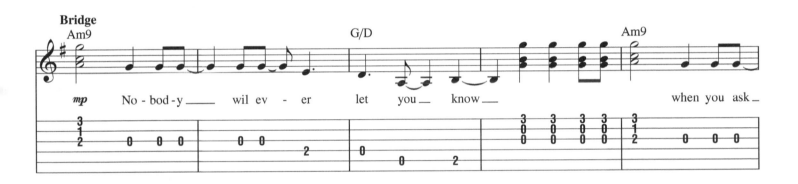

mp No-bod-y ___ wil ev-er let you ___ know ___ when you ask ___

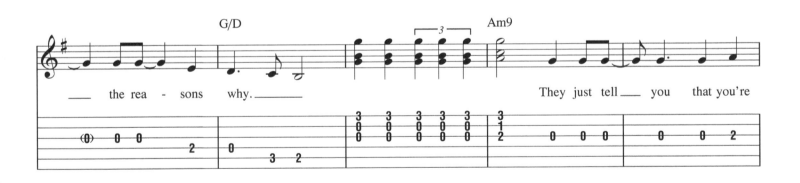

___ the rea-sons why.___ They just tell ___ you that you're

on your ___ own, ___ fill your head ___ all full of ___ lies.___

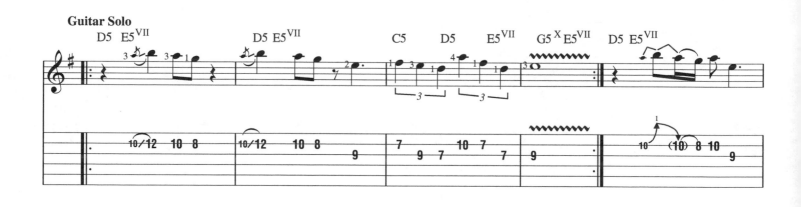

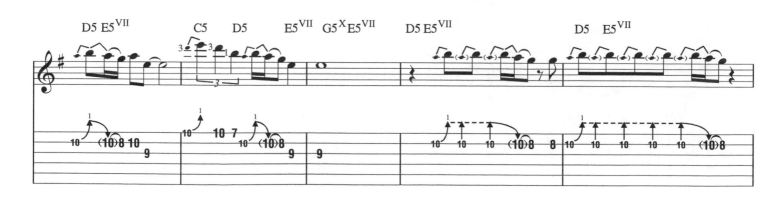

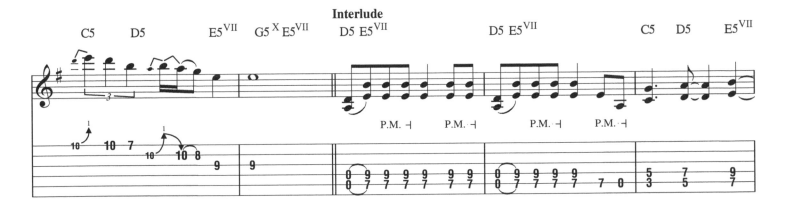

Interlude

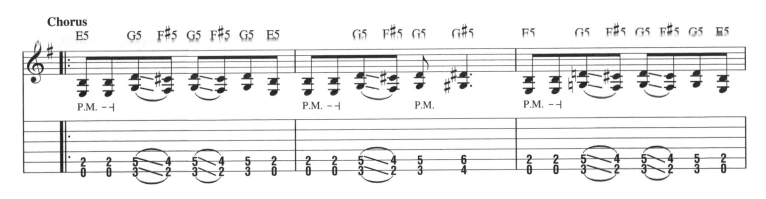

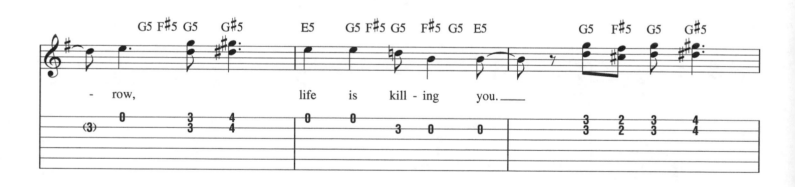

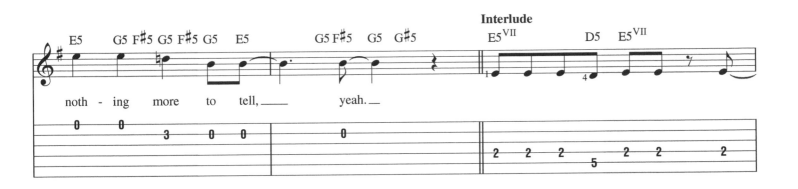

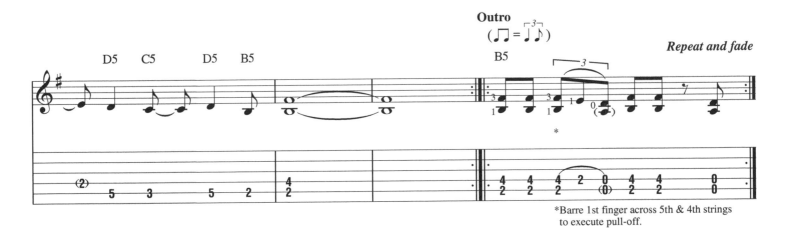

*Barre 1st finger across 5th & 4th strings
to execute pull-off.

Additional Lyrics

2. The people who have crippled you,
You wanna see them burn.
The gates of life are closed on you
And there's just no return.
You're wishing that the hands of doom
Could take your mind away,
And you don't care if you don't see
Again the light of day.

Chorus Ev'rything around you
What's it coming to?
God knows as your dog knows,
Bog blast all of you.
Sabbath, bloody sabbath,
Nothing more to do.
Living just for dying,
Dying just for you, yeah.

Supernaut

Words and Music by Frank Iommi, Terence Butler, William Ward and John Osbourne

Strum Pattern: 2, 3

Verse

1. I want to reach out and touch the sky. ___ I want to touch the sun, but I ___
2., 3. *See additional lyrics*

___ don't need to fly. ___ I'm gon - na climb up ev - 'ry moun-tain on the moon, ___

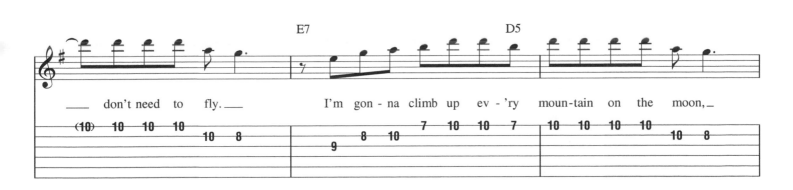

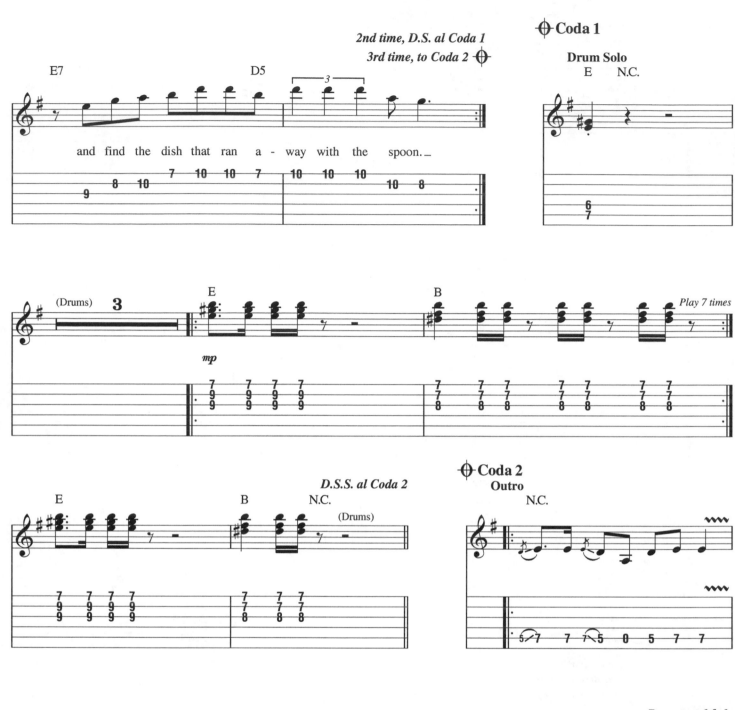

and find the dish that ran a - way with the spoon.

Additional Lyrics

2. I've crossed the oceans,
Turned ev'ry bend.
I found the crossing
Near the golden rainbow's end.
I've been through magic
And through life's reality.
I've lived a thousand years,
It never bothered me.

3. Got no religion,
Don't need no friends.
Got all I want
And I don't need to pretend.
Don't try to reach me
'Cause I'll tear up your mind.
I've seen the future
And I've left it behind.

War Pigs (Interpolating Luke's Wall)

Words and Music by Frank Iommi, John Osbourne, William Ward and Terence Butler

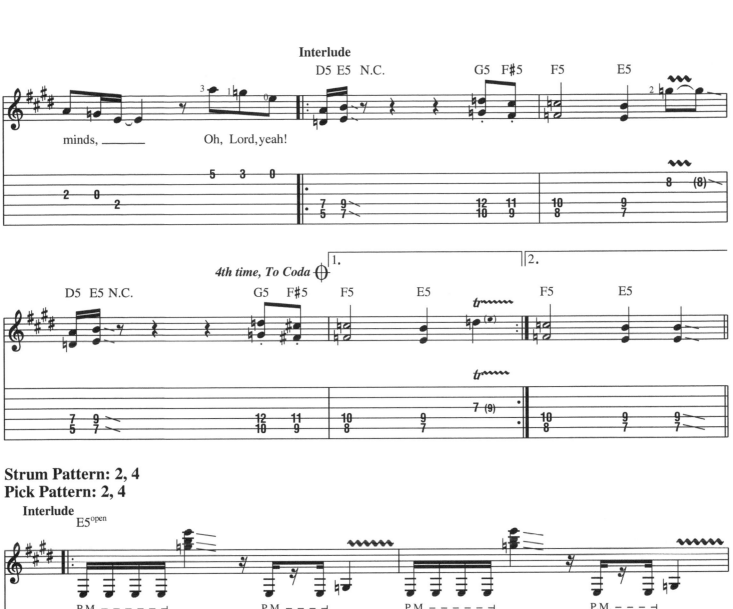

Interlude

minds, _____ Oh, Lord, yeah!

4th time, To Coda

Strum Pattern: 2, 4
Pick Pattern: 2, 4

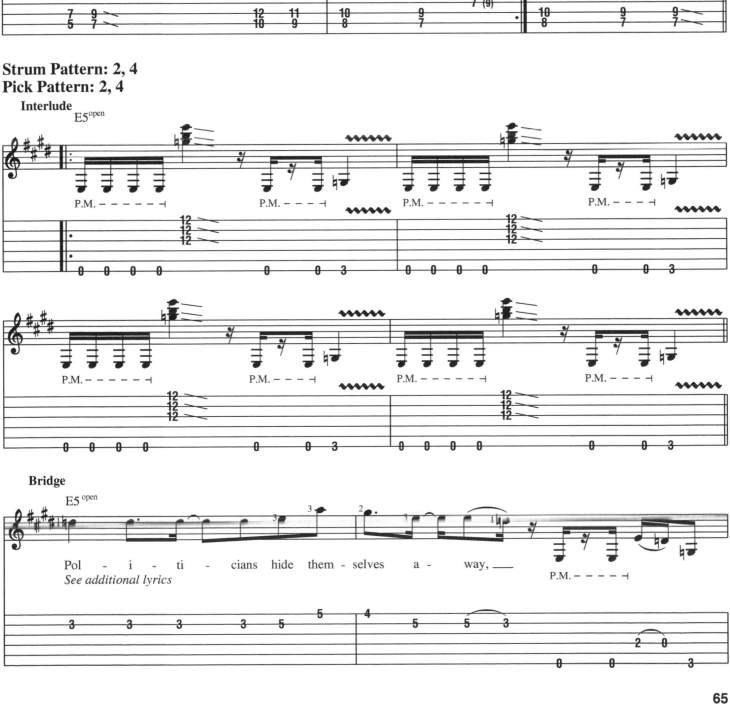

Interlude

E5 open

Bridge

E5 open

Pol - i - ti - cians hide them - selves a - way, ____

See additional lyrics

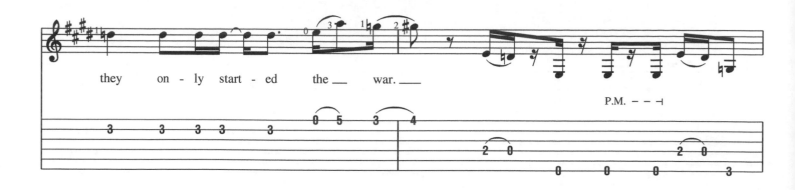

they   on - ly   start - ed   the — war. —

P.M. – – –

Why   should   they —   go   out —   to ———— fight? —

Interlude

D5 E5 N.C.   G5 F#5

They   leave   that — all   to   the   poor! —   Yeah.

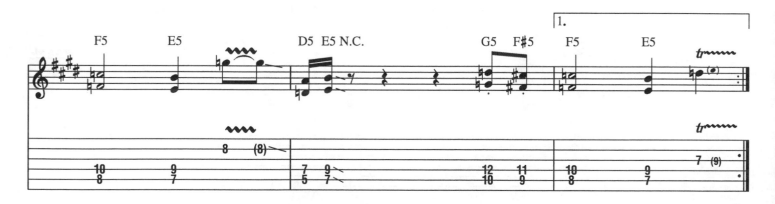

1.

F5   E5   D5 E5 N.C.   G5 F#5   F5   E5

2.

Guitar Solo

F5   E5   E5 open

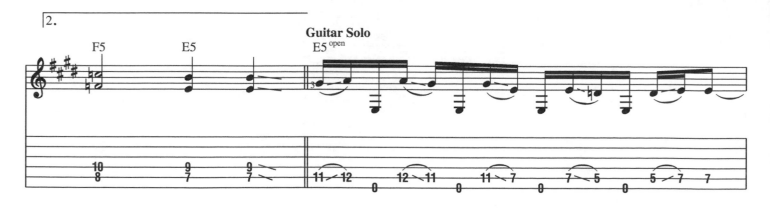

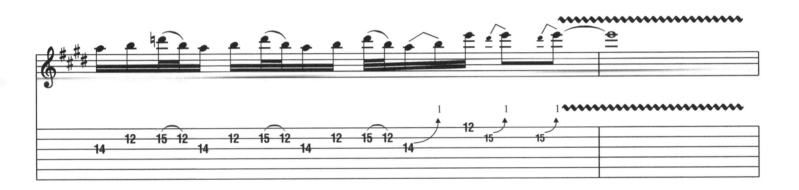

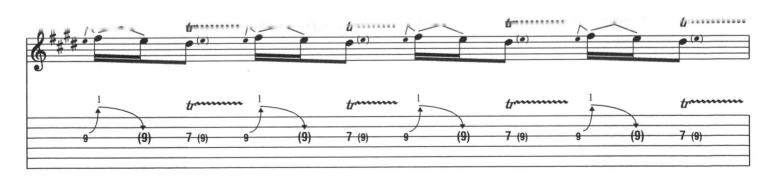

D.C. al Coda
(take repeat)

⊕ Coda

Interlude (Luke's Wall)

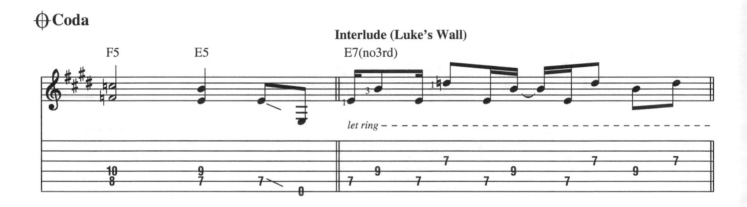

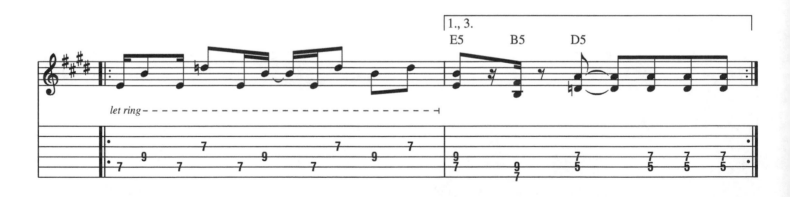

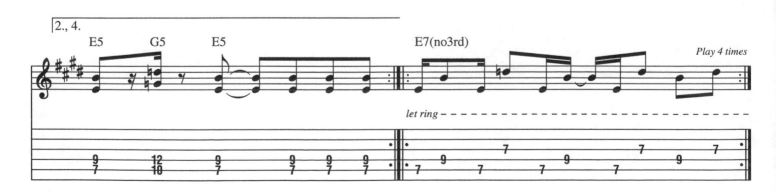

Additional Lyrics

2. Now in darkness, world stops turning,
   Ashes where the bodies burning.
   No more war pigs have the power.
   Hand of God has struck the hour.
   Day of judgment, God is calling,
   On their knees, the war pigs crawling.
   Begging mercies for their sins,
   Satan laughing, spreads his wings.
   Oh, Lord, yeah!

Bridge Time will tell on their power minds,
   Making war just for fun.
   Treating people just like pawns in chess,
   Wait till their judgment day comes.
   Yeah.

Sweet Leaf

Words and Music by Frank Iommi, John Osbourne, William Ward and Terence Butler

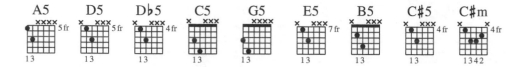

Strum Pattern: 2, 3
Pick Pattern: 1, 3

*V th position

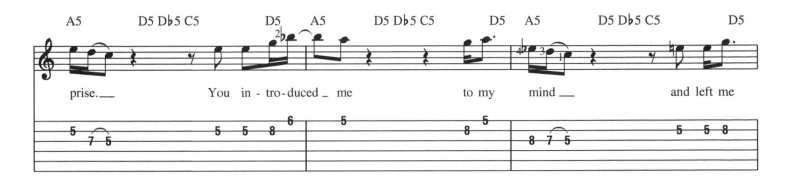

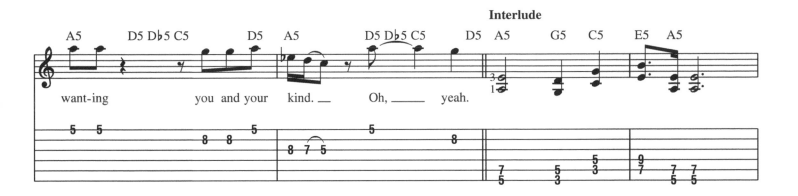

Interlude

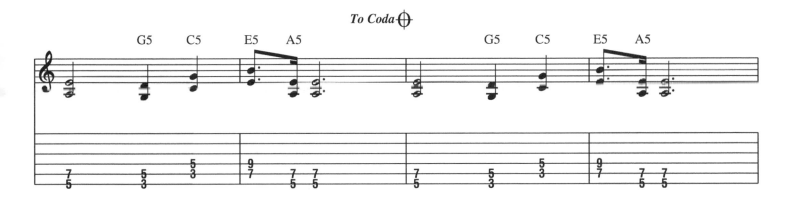

To Coda ⊕

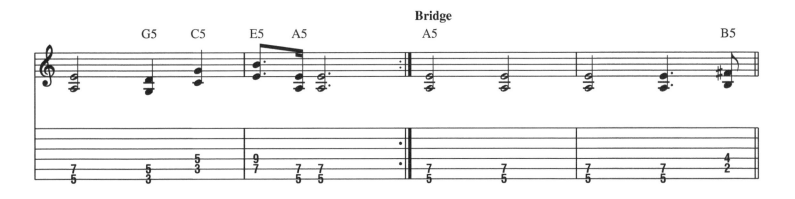

Bridge

Faster

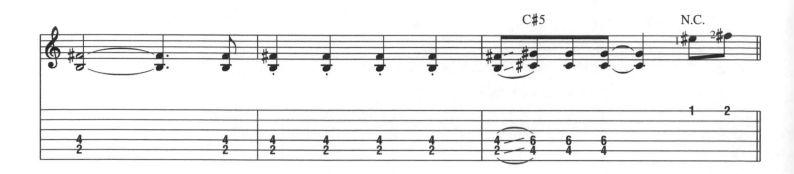

Guitar Solo

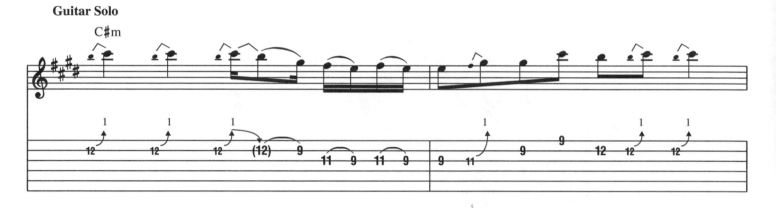

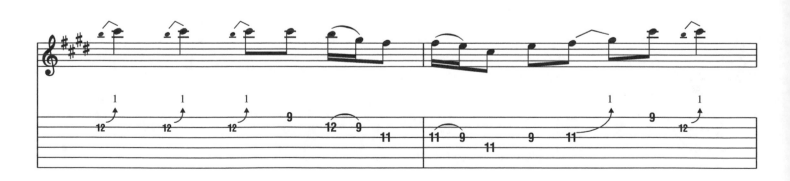

D.C. al Coda

Interlude

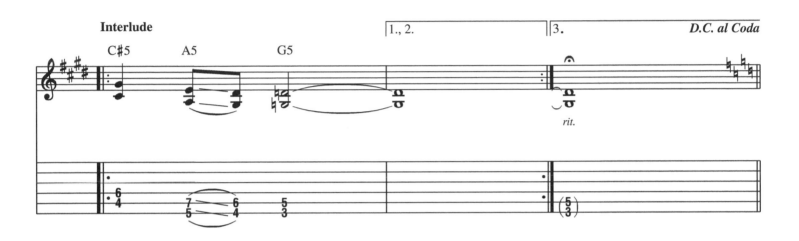

Coda

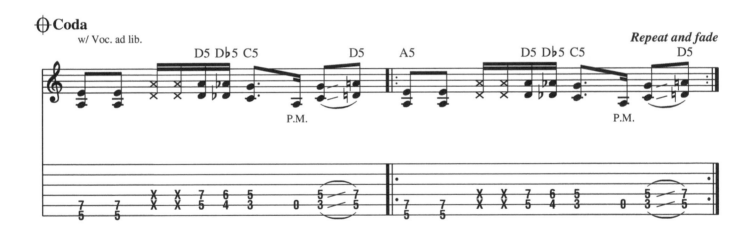

Repeat and fade

Additional Lyrics

2. My life was empty, forever on a down.
   Until you took me, showed me around.
   My life is free now, my life is clear.
   I love you sweet leaf, though you can't hear.

3. Straight people don't know what you're about.
   They put you down and shut you out.
   You gave to me a new belief.
   And soon the world will love you, sweet leaf.

The Wizard

Words and Music by Frank Iommi, Terence Butler, William Ward and John Osbourne

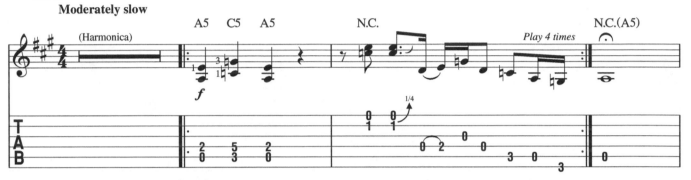

Strum Pattern: 4, 5

Intro

Moderately slow

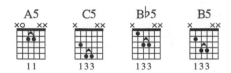

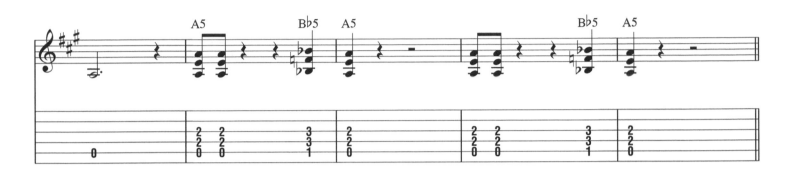

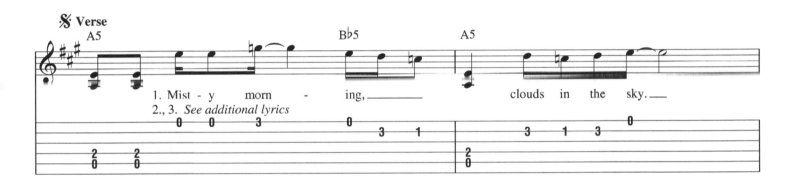

1. Mist - y morn - ing, _____ clouds in the sky. _____
2., 3. *See additional lyrics*

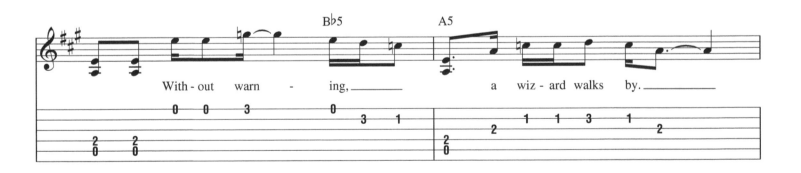

With - out warn - ing, _____ a wiz - ard walks by. _____

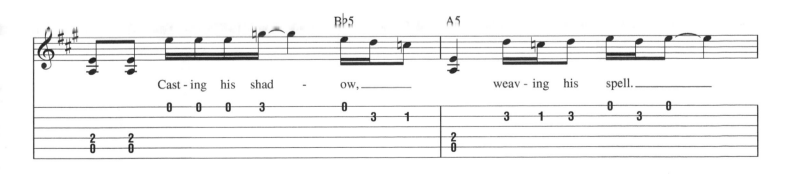

Cast - ing his shad - ow, _____ weav - ing his spell. _____

Long grey cloak,_____ twin - kl - ing bell.___

Chorus

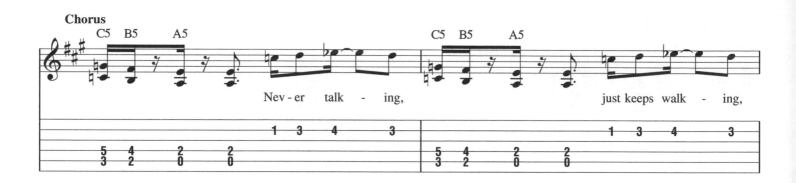

Nev - er talk - ing, just keeps walk - ing,

3rd time, to Coda ⊕

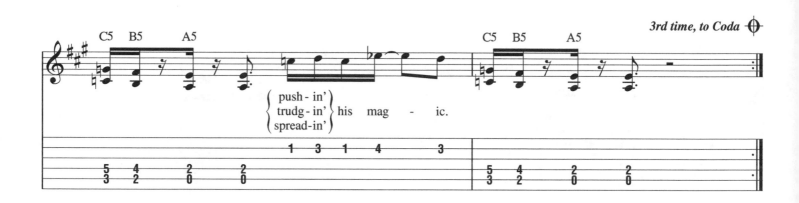

{ push - in'
  trudg - in' } his mag - ic.
  spread-in' }

Guitar Solo

Additional Lyrics

2. Evil power disappears.
   Demons worry when the wizard is near.
   He turns tears into joy.
   Ev'ryone's happy when the wizard walks by.

3. Sun is shinin', clouds have gone by.
   All the people give a happy sigh.
   He has passed by, giving his sign,
   Left all the people feelin' so fine.

This series features simplified arrangements with notes, tab, chord charts, and strum and pick patterns.

MIXED FOLIOS

00702287 Acoustic	$19.99
00702002 Acoustic Rock Hits for Easy Guitar	$15.99
00702166 All-Time Best Guitar Collection	$19.99
00702232 Best Acoustic Songs for Easy Guitar	$16.99
00119835 Best Children's Songs	$16.99
00703055 The Big Book of Nursery Rhymes & Children's Songs	$16.99
00698978 Big Christmas Collection	$19.99
00702394 Bluegrass Songs for Easy Guitar	$15.99
00289632 Bohemian Rhapsody	$19.99
00703387 Celtic Classics	$16.99
00224808 Chart Hits of 2016-2017	$14.99
00267383 Chart Hits of 2017-2018	$14.99
00334293 Chart Hits of 2019-2020	$16.99
00403479 Chart Hits of 2021-2022	$16.99
00702149 Children's Christian Songbook	$9.99
00702028 Christmas Classics	$8.99
00101779 Christmas Guitar	$14.99
00702141 Classic Rock	$8.95
00159642 Classical Melodies	$12.99
00253933 Disney/Pixar's Coco	$16.99
00702203 CMT's 100 Greatest Country Songs	$34.99
00702283 The Contemporary Christian Collection	$16.99

00196954 Contemporary Disney	$19.99
00702239 Country Classics for Easy Guitar	$24.99
00702257 Easy Acoustic Guitar Songs	$17.99
00702041 Favorite Hymns for Easy Guitar	$12.99
00222701 Folk Pop Songs	$17.99
00126894 Frozen	$14.99
00333922 Frozen 2	$14.99
00702286 Glee	$16.99
00702160 The Great American Country Songbook	$19.99
00702148 Great American Gospel for Guitar	$14.99
00702050 Great Classical Themes for Easy Guitar	$9.99
00275088 The Greatest Showman	$17.99
00148030 Halloween Guitar Songs	$14.99
00702273 Irish Songs	$14.99
00192503 Jazz Classics for Easy Guitar	$16.99
00702275 Jazz Favorites for Easy Guitar	$17.99
00702274 Jazz Standards for Easy Guitar	$19.99
00702162 Jumbo Easy Guitar Songbook	$24.99
00232285 La La Land	$16.99
00702258 Legends of Rock	$14.99
00702189 MTV's 100 Greatest Pop Songs	$34.99
00702272 1950s Rock	$16.99
00702271 1960s Rock	$16.99
00702270 1970s Rock	$24.99
00702269 1980s Rock	$16.99

00702268 1990s Rock	$24.99
00369043 Rock Songs for Kids	$14.99
00109725 Once	$14.99
00702187 Selections from O Brother Where Art Thou?	$19.99
00702178 100 Songs for Kids	$16.99
00702515 Pirates of the Caribbean	$17.99
00702125 Praise and Worship for Guitar	$14.99
00287930 Songs from *A Star Is Born, The Greatest Showman, La La Land,* and More Movie Musicals	$16.99
00702285 Southern Rock Hits	$12.99
00156420 Star Wars Music	$16.99
00121535 30 Easy Celtic Guitar Solos	$16.99
00244654 Top Hits of 2017	$14.99
00283786 Top Hits of 2018	$14.99
00302269 Top Hits of 2019	$14.99
00355779 Top Hits of 2020	$14.99
00374083 Top Hits of 2021	$16.99
00702294 Top Worship Hits	$17.99
00702255 VH1's 100 Greatest Hard Rock Songs	$34.99
00702175 VH1's 100 Greatest Songs of Rock and Roll	$34.99
00702253 Wicked	$12.99

ARTIST COLLECTIONS

00702267 AC/DC for Easy Guitar	$16.99
00156221 Adele – 25	$16.99
00396889 Adele – 30	$19.99
00702040 Best of the Allman Brothers	$16.99
00702865 J.S. Bach for Easy Guitar	$15.99
00702169 Best of The Beach Boys	$16.99
00702292 The Beatles — 1	$22.99
00125796 Best of Chuck Berry	$16.99
00702201 The Essential Black Sabbath	$15.99
00702250 blink-182 — Greatest Hits	$17.99
02501615 Zac Brown Band — The Foundation	$17.99
02501621 Zac Brown Band — You Get What You Give	$16.99
00702043 Best of Johnny Cash	$17.99
00702090 Eric Clapton's Best	$16.99
00702086 Eric Clapton — from the Album Unplugged	$17.99
00702202 The Essential Eric Clapton	$17.99
00702053 Best of Patsy Cline	$17.99
00222697 Very Best of Coldplay – 2nd Edition	$17.99
00702229 The Very Best of Creedence Clearwater Revival	$16.99
00702145 Best of Jim Croce	$16.99
00702278 Crosby, Stills & Nash	$12.99
14042809 Bob Dylan	$15.99
00702276 Fleetwood Mac — Easy Guitar Collection	$17.99
00139462 The Very Best of Grateful Dead	$16.99
00702136 Best of Merle Haggard	$16.99
00702227 Jimi Hendrix — Smash Hits	$19.99
00702288 Best of Hillsong United	$12.99
00702236 Best of Antonio Carlos Jobim	$15.99

00702245 Elton John — Greatest Hits 1970–2002	$19.99
00129855 Jack Johnson	$17.99
00702204 Robert Johnson	$16.99
00702234 Selections from Toby Keith — 35 Biggest Hits	$12.95
00702003 Kiss	$16.99
00702216 Lynyrd Skynyrd	$17.99
00702182 The Essential Bob Marley	$16.99
00146081 Maroon 5	$14.99
00121925 Bruno Mars — Unorthodox Jukebox	$12.99
00702248 Paul McCartney — All the Best	$14.99
00125484 The Best of MercyMe	$12.99
00702209 Steve Miller Band — Young Hearts (Greatest Hits)	$12.95
00124167 Jason Mraz	$15.99
00702096 Best of Nirvana	$16.99
00702211 The Offspring — Greatest Hits	$17.99
00138026 One Direction	$17.99
00702030 Best of Roy Orbison	$17.99
00702144 Best of Ozzy Osbourne	$14.99
00702279 Tom Petty	$17.99
00102911 Pink Floyd	$17.99
00702139 Elvis Country Favorites	$19.99
00702293 The Very Best of Prince	$19.99
00699415 Best of Queen for Guitar	$16.99
00109279 Best of R.E.M.	$14.99
00702208 Red Hot Chili Peppers — Greatest Hits	$17.99
00198960 The Rolling Stones	$17.99
00174793 The Very Best of Santana	$16.99
00702196 Best of Bob Seger	$16.99
00146046 Ed Sheeran	$17.99

00702252 Frank Sinatra — Nothing But the Best	$12.99
00702010 Best of Rod Stewart	$17.99
00702049 Best of George Strait	$17.99
00702259 Taylor Swift for Easy Guitar	$15.99
00359800 Taylor Swift – Easy Guitar Anthology	$24.99
00702260 Taylor Swift — Fearless	$14.99
00139727 Taylor Swift — 1989	$19.99
00115960 Taylor Swift — Red	$16.99
00253667 Taylor Swift — Reputation	$17.99
00702290 Taylor Swift — Speak Now	$16.99
00232849 Chris Tomlin Collection – 2nd Edition	$14.99
00702226 Chris Tomlin — See the Morning	$12.95
00148643 Train	$14.99
00702427 U2 — 18 Singles	$19.99
00702108 Best of Stevie Ray Vaughan	$17.99
00279005 The Who	$14.99
00702123 Best of Hank Williams	$15.99
00194548 Best of John Williams	$14.99
00702228 Neil Young — Greatest Hits	$17.99
00119133 Neil Young — Harvest	$14.99

Prices, contents and availability subject to change without notice.

Visit Hal Leonard online at **halleonard.com**

HAL·LEONARD GUITAR PLAY-ALONG

Complete song lists available online.

This series will help you play your favorite songs quickly and easily. Just follow the tab and listen to the audio to the hear how the guitar should sound, and then play along using the separate backing tracks. Audio files also include software to slow down the tempo without changing pitch. The melody and lyrics are included in the book so that you can sing or simply follow along.

INCLUDES TAB

Prices, contents, and availability subject to change without notice.

HAL·LEONARD®
www.halleonard.com

Get Better at Guitar

...with these Great Guitar Instruction Books from Hal Leonard!

101 GUITAR TIPS
INCLUDES TAB

STUFF ALL THE PROS KNOW AND USE

by Adam St. James

This book contains invaluable guidance on everything from scales and music theory to truss rod adjustments, proper recording studio set-ups, and much more.

00695737 Book/Online Audio $17.99

AMAZING PHRASING
INCLUDES TAB

by Tom Kolb

This book/audio pack explores all the main components necessary for crafting well-balanced rhythmic and melodic phrases. It also explains how these phrases are put together to form cohesive solos. The companion audio contains 89 demo tracks, most with full-band backing.

00695583 Book/Online Audio $22.99

ARPEGGIOS FOR THE MODERN GUITARIST
INCLUDES TAB

by Tom Kolb

Using this no-nonsense book with online audio, guitarists will learn to apply and execute all types of arpeggio forms using a variety of techniques, including alternate picking, sweep picking, tapping, string skipping, and legato.

00695862 Book/Online Audio $22.99

BLUES YOU CAN USE

by John Ganapes

This comprehensive source for learning blues guitar is designed to develop both your lead and rhythm playing. Includes: 21 complete solos • blues chords, progressions and riffs • turnarounds • movable scales and soloing techniques • string bending • utilizing the entire fingerboard • and more.

00142420 Book/Online Media..................$22.99

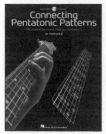

CONNECTING PENTATONIC PATTERNS
INCLUDES TAB

by Tom Kolb

If you've been finding yourself trapped in the pentatonic box, this book is for you! This hands-on book with online audio offers examples for guitar players of all levels, from beginner to advanced. Study this book faithfully, and soon you'll be soloing all over the neck with the greatest of ease.

00696445 Book/Online Audio $24.99

FRETBOARD MASTERY
INCLUDES TAB

by Troy Stetina

Untangle the mysterious regions of the guitar fretboard and unlock your potential. This book familiarizes you with all the shapes you need to know by applying them in real musical examples, thereby reinforcing and reaffirming your newfound knowledge.

00695331 Book/Online Audio $22.99

GUITAR AEROBICS
INCLUDES TAB

by Troy Nelson

Here is a daily dose of guitar "vitamins" to keep your chops fine tuned! Musical styles include rock, blues, jazz, metal, country, and funk. Techniques taught include alternate picking, arpeggios, sweep picking, string skipping, legato, string bending, and rhythm guitar.

00695946 Book/Online Audio $24.99

GUITAR CLUES
INCLUDES TAB

OPERATION PENTATONIC

by Greg Koch

Whether you're new to improvising or have been doing it for a while, this book/audio pack will provide loads of delicious licks and tricks that you can use right away, from volume swells and chicken pickin' to intervallic and chordal ideas.

00695827 Book/Online Audio $19.99

PAT METHENY – GUITAR ETUDES
INCLUDES TAB

Over the years, in many master classes and workshops around the world, Pat has demonstrated the kind of daily workout he puts himself through. This book includes a collection of 14 guitar etudes he created to help you limber up, improve picking technique and build finger independence.

00696587 ....$17.99

PICTURE CHORD ENCYCLOPEDIA

This comprehensive guitar chord resource for all playing styles and levels features five voicings of 44 chord qualities for all twelve keys – 2,640 chords in all! For each, there is a clearly illustrated chord frame, as well as *an actual photo* of the chord being played!.

00695224 ....$22.99

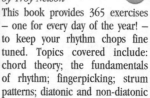

RHYTHM GUITAR 365
INCLUDES TAB

by Troy Nelson

This book provides 365 exercises – one for every day of the year! – to keep your rhythm chops fine tuned. Topics covered include: chord theory; the fundamentals of rhythm; fingerpicking; strum patterns; diatonic and non-diatonic progressions; triads; major and minor keys; and more.

00103627 Book/Online Audio $27.99

SCALE CHORD RELATIONSHIPS
INCLUDES TAB

by Michael Mueller & Jeff Schroedl

This book/audio pack explains how to: recognize keys • analyze chord progressions • use the modes • play over nondiatonic harmony • use harmonic and melodic minor scales • use symmetrical scales • incorporate exotic scales • and much more!

00695563 Book/Online Audio $17.99

SPEED MECHANICS FOR LEAD GUITAR
INCLUDES TAB

by Troy Stetina

Take your playing to the stratosphere with this advanced lead book which will help you develop speed and precision in today's explosive playing styles. Learn the fastest ways to achieve speed and control, secrets to make your practice time really count, and how to open your ears and make your musical ideas more solid and tangible.

00699323 Book/Online Audio $22.99

TOTAL ROCK GUITAR
INCLUDES TAB

by Troy Stetina

This comprehensive source for learning rock guitar is designed to develop both your lead and rhythm playing. It covers: getting a tone that rocks • open chords, power chords and barre chords • riffs, scales and licks • string bending, strumming, and harmonics • and more.

00695246 Book/Online Audio $22.99

Guitar World Presents STEVE VAI'S GUITAR WORKOUT
INCLUDES TAB

In this book, Steve Vai reveals his path to virtuoso enlightenment with two challenging guitar workouts – one 10-hour and one 30-hour – which include scale and chord exercises, ear training, sight-reading, music theory, and much more.

00119643..................$16.99

HAL•LEONARD®

Order these and more publications from your favorite music retailer at

halleonard.com

Prices, contents, and availability subject to change without notice.

0322
032